Learning Theology

Learning Theology

Tracking the Spirit of Christian Faith

Amos Yong

WESTMINSTER
JOHN KNOX PRESS
LOUISVILLE · KENTUCKY

© 2018 Amos Yong

First edition
Published by Westminster John Knox Press
Louisville, Kentucky

18 19 20 21 22 23 24 25 26 27—10 9 8 7 6 5 4 3 2 1

Unless otherwise indicated, Scripture quotations are from the New Revised Standard Version of the Bible, copyright © 1989 by the Division of Christian Education of the National Council of the Churches of Christ in the U.S.A., and are used by permission. NET = New English Translation. CEB = Common English Bible.

Book design by Sharon Adams
Cover design by Mark Abrams

Library of Congress Cataloging-in-Publication Data

Names: Yong, Amos, author.
Title: Learning theology : tracking the spirit of Christian faith / Amos Yong.
Description: First edition. | Louisville, Kentucky : Westminster John Knox Press, 2018. |
    Includes bibliographical references and index.
Identifiers: LCCN 2018012522 (print) | LCCN 2018015772 (ebook) |
    ISBN 9781611648805 (ebk.) | ISBN 9780664263966 (pbk. : alk. paper)
Subjects: LCSH: Theology.
Classification: LCC BR118 (ebook) | LCC BR118 .Y665 2018 (print) | DDC 230—dc23
LC record available at https://lccn.loc.gov/2018012522

To

James H. Barnes III,

Paul R. Eddy, and

John Herzog—

exemplary teachers, mentors, and colleagues

Contents

Preface   xi

Introduction: What Is a Theologian?   1

   Macrina as Lay Theologian   2

   Thomas Aquinas as Classical (Professional) Theologian   4

   John Wesley as Pastoral and Practical Theologian   6

   You and I as Those Who Love God and Want to Know
      and Serve God   8

Part I   The Sources of Theology

1. Scripture: The Word and Breath of God   15

   1.1   Behind of the Text   16

   1.2   The World of the Text   18

   1.3   In Front of the Text   20

   1.4   The Spirit of the Text   22

2. Tradition: The Living Body of Christ and the Fellowship
   of the Holy Spirit   27

   2.1   Church and Tradition: Charisma and Institution   28

   2.2   The Spirit/s of Protestantism   30

   2.3   The Church Catholic as the Fellowship of the Spirit   33

   2.4   The Spirit of Tradition in Its Contextuality   35

3. Reason: Renewing the Mind in the Spirit   39

   3.1   Rationality as Traditioned   40

3.2   Scientific Revolution, the Enlightenment,
       and Universal Reason   42

3.3   Postmodern (Ir)Rationalities(!)   45

3.4   The Reasoning Spirit   48

4. Experience: Life in, by, and through the Spirit   53

4.1   Socialization   54

4.2   Intersectionality   56

4.3   Encountering the Living God, Experiencing Redemption   59

4.4   The Fullness of the Spirit and the Life of the Mind   61

Part II   The Practices of Theology

5. Theology as Spiritual Practice: What Difference Does
    It Make in Personal Lives?   67

5.1   Knowing and Loving God   68

5.2   Loving and Serving Our Neighbors   70

5.3   Discerning the Spirit   72

5.4   Eschatological Rationality   74

6. Theology as Ecclesial Practice: By, for, and through
    the Church   77

6.1   The Church as One: Dogmatic Identity
       and Ecclesial Unity   78

6.2   The Church as Holy: The Social Distinctiveness
       of the Ecclesia   80

6.3   The Church as Catholic: Global Cultures
       and Ecclesial Witness   83

6.4   The Church as Apostolic: The Many Tongues
       of the Spirit's Mission   85

7. Theology as Scholarly Practice: Researching, Writing,
    and Studying Theology   89

7.1   The Initial Contexts of (Undergraduate) Theologizing   90

7.2   The Theological Research Paper or Project   92

7.3   Theological Integration and the Christian University   94

7.4   Theologizing as a Spiritual Discipline   96

8. Theology as Charismatic Practice: Theology
   by the Spirit, Trinitarian Theologians   101

   8.1   Starting with the Spirit   102

   8.2   Theologizing after Easter and after Pentecost   103

   8.3   Pentecostal Perspective, Trinitarian Theologian   105

   8.4   The Spirit Has the First, Initiating Word   107

Appendix   Becoming a Professional Theologian:
            Getting There from Here   111

Discerning the Call to Graduate/Doctoral
            Theological Education   111

Welcome to the Guild/s   113

Navigating Graduate School   115

The Spirit and the Intellectual Vocation   117

Acknowledgments   121

Glossary   123

Index of Scripture   131

Index of Subjects and Names   133

Preface

I have written this book for first-year theology students, whoever they might be and wherever they might be. I have in mind especially undergraduate students in Christian colleges and universities, including those affiliated with the Council for Christian Colleges and Universities yet also those enrolled in tertiary programs of study at institutions historically affiliated with mainline Protestant denominations. My primarily intended readers are not only those in their first introduction to theology/doctrine courses but also those intrigued by theology and certainly those who are thinking about majoring in theology. At the same time, I think first-year seminarians might also benefit from this book, particularly those without any theological study in their background, although a liberal arts undergraduate education helps. Last but not least, I am hoping that lay reading groups in local churches, congregations, or communities might find this a helpful primer to catalyze their own self-understanding as theologians.

An introduction urging that even theological neophytes are theologians opens up to the two parts of the book, each with four chapters. Part I focuses on the "sources" of theology and is structured around the so-called Wesleyan quadrilateral of Scripture, tradition, reason, and experience. The second part discusses the "practices" for young and aspiring theologians: spiritual, ecclesial, and practical (for undergraduate-level theological aspirants). The final chapter of this book brings to culmination and further unpacks the major thread across the eight chapters: that all theologians write as persons of the Spirit, in the shadow not just of Easter, but also of Pentecost. In short, *Learning Theology: Tracking the Spirit* analyzes the sources and practices of the theological endeavor as *pneumatically* charged—related to life in the Spirit and to the empowerment of the Spirit in the pursuit and development of the life of the mind—in ways relevant to Christian existence in the present time and world.

Each of the eight main chapters in the two parts of the book will conclude with a few discussion questions and a "further reading" list of about a dozen or so volumes (no overall bibliography is given at the end). The work includes sidebars. And an appendix discusses graduate theological education and the pursuit of professional theologizing for those who might become open to considering such a vocation. There are no footnotes or endnotes, although a glossary is included to facilitate easy reference to the more technical terms needed to present a fuller account of the issues we are traversing.

Faculty who assign this volume in their theology courses: thank you! Surely you will have your own ideas on everything included on the following pages. My goal is not to prescribe to impressionable young minds that there is only one way to do theology, but to open up the theological highway and encourage students to take it. Whether they embark on this lifelong endeavor after the semester will depend on our collaborative endeavor, but more so on your living and personal example (no pressure though!). I have tried my best to make this book as accessible as possible to your students, but I realize my limitations and am thankful for your help in this process toward our mutual goals: that young theologians might be inspired and launched.

Pasadena, California
first week of the autumnal equinox, 2017

Introduction

What Is a Theologian?

The word *theology* comes from the Greek *theos*, meaning "God," and *logos*, denoting "a field, area, or topic of study": in compound for "the study of God." This might seem presumptuous for our puny human minds. Doesn't the Bible itself say, "For my thoughts are not your thoughts, nor are your ways my ways, says the LORD. For as the heavens are higher than the earth, so are my ways higher than your ways and my thoughts than your thoughts" (Isa. 55:8–9)? So how can God even be studied?

To answer that question, we begin by introducing three theologians: Macrina, the older sister of the Cappadocian brothers, as a lay theologian; Thomas Aquinas as the classic example of what we might call a professional theologian; and John Wesley as a practical theologian. There is more than one way to study God as a theologian, we shall see. If you are just starting out in theological studies, our goal in these introductory pages is to make it possible for you to imagine yourself as a theologian. For starters, we will define a theologian as someone who thinks about and considers God, and all things in relationship to God. What kind of theologian you end up becoming in the shorter or longer term, even after you have completed this initial course of study, is not only up to you but in many ways remains unpredictable, as we shall discover. But the key to the success you will experience by the grace of God is to be open to becoming a student of things divine, however young or more mature you might be!

1

Macrina as Lay Theologian

Saint Macrina is often indicated as "the Younger" (324–379) in order to differentiate her from her grandmother, Saint Macrina the Elder (ca. 270–ca. 340). The latter's son, Basil the Elder (d. 379), had nine or ten children, including Macrina the Younger (the firstborn) and her two brothers, Saint Basil of Caesarea (329/330–379) and Saint Gregory of Nyssa (ca. 335–ca. 395). These brothers, along with their friend, Gregory of Nazianzus (329–390), also known as Gregory the Theologian, are renowned collectively as the Cappadocian Fathers (Cappadocia being the region in modern-day Turkey where they resided, ministered, and worked). The fame of these Cappadocians sometimes leaves Macrina the Younger's legacy obscure, although it is also largely due to her brother Gregory that we know what we do about his eldest sibling.

Gregory's *Life of St. Macrina* (*Vita Sanctae Macrinæ*) was written not too long after his sister's death. In it, he recounts her spiritual journey based on conversations at her deathbed. When the young man to whom she was pledged died unexpectedly, Macrina resolved to remain faithful to that betrothal as if married. Following her father's passing shortly thereafter, she as oldest child committed herself to helping her siblings by serving as their tutor and by ordering her mother's affairs. Through this experience, as well as suffering the loss of her younger brother Naucratius to an inexplicable hunting accident, Macrina learned to harness her own fleshly passions and desires, and she encouraged her mother to do likewise. Rather than pursuing a classical education, Macrina saturated herself in the Scriptures and constantly recited the Psalms, which became her constant companion. Macrina devoted herself to an ascetic and monastic lifestyle, and soon a small convent gathered around her as others were drawn by her example. If Saint Antony the Great (251–356) was the model monk of the early church, enshrined as such by Saint Athanasius's life story of this desert ascetic, then Macrina is remembered as the archetypal nun.

By all conventional standards, Macrina would not have made history as a theologian: she was a nun (rather than monk), ran a monastery convent for women (rather than spending time studying or mastering the classical tradition), and did not write anything—or did she? While on her deathbed, her brother Gregory recorded what he presents as an extended conversation with his sister, which he then published as *On the Soul and Resurrection* (*De anima et resurrectione*). These dialogues seem to be fashioned after both philosophical and theological predecessors. With regard to the former, Gregory's questions are answered by Macrina as Plato's were by Socrates (in the *Phaedo*, a text focused also on the immortality of the soul, articulated at the latter's deathbed). With regard to the latter theological tradition, however, an inversion occurs: Macrina is the virgin philosopher-theologian whose wisdom and sound teaching Gregory preserves, but this reverses the model presented in the (apocryphal) *Acts of Paul and Thecla*, about the virgin young woman who was commissioned to continue and extend the apostle Paul's ministry. Thus Gregory is distraught by his brother Basil's recent death and seeks comfort from his sister and teacher (as he calls her). He presents his doubts about the persistence of the soul upon the death of the body, is apprehensive about death, and worries about the impossibility, or improbability, of the resurrection of the body and the soul's postmortem fate. On each point, Macrina presents counterconsiderations, often buttressed and undergirded by Scripture. She explicates the nature of the soul, gives reasons for its endurance in Hades through bodily death, and anticipates the body's eventual resurrection (here contrary to the Platonic dialogues). The resurrection conjoins the body with the soul as in the original conception and in accordance with their primordial human

> *Macrina put theological reflection and teaching in service of Christian life.*

union manifest in the Genesis narrative. All the while Macrina clarifies how the human soul is somehow divine but nevertheless creaturely and thereby unlike the Deity. Crucial in *On the Soul and Resurrection*, however, is that such deliberation about the destiny of the soul is not for the sake of speculation but for that of sanctification: to enable purification of human hearts from the carnality that can inhibit the resurrection to eternal life.

Clearly, Macrina herself wrote nothing, like Jesus. Yet, even if her authorship of *On the Soul and the Resurrection* is unconfirmable, the teachings in this treatise attributed to her left a deep impression on her brother. At the least, they led him to depict her as teacher, in fact, as *the* teacher for the group that has come to be known as the Cappadocian theologians. Further, although not classically trained, Macrina is represented as a clear and analytical thinker. But Macrina is spiritually devout, even as she is remembered as a positive model of the ascetic life. Her philosophical and theological argumentation is put in service of scriptural faith and, more importantly, of the redemption of the souls and the quest for holiness. She did not set out to pursue the theological life of the mind, yet she will be remembered at least in part for her theological rigor and clarity of thought.

Similarly, most first-year theology students today do not anticipate becoming professional theologians. Still, our commitment to the service of Christ, rather than being devoid of theological ideas, will actually be sustained and empowered by them. At the end of her life, Macrina's spiritual passions were transformed into theological ruminations about the destiny of human souls, specifically about our hoped-for union with the Creator God. In a similar way, even if we never consider writing a theological treatise, our lives as followers of Jesus will leave a legacy and witness. Perhaps we will be remembered for our theological beliefs, even if we never aspired for theological recognition.

Thomas Aquinas as Classical (Professional) Theologian

Born to Landolph the count of Aquino in the 1220s, Thomas entered the Dominican Order in 1244 and was then sent to study with its foremost theologian and prominent Aristotelian scholar, Albert the Great (1205–80). Initially quiet, unassuming, and unimpressive to his peers, he was known among them as "the dumb ox." But his intellectual capacities were nonetheless noticed by his teacher. Ordained in 1251/1252, he began lecturing shortly thereafter. Over the next two decades Thomas was a prolific writer, authoring over one hundred texts. Near the end of his life, he was caught up in controversies within the church about the role of Aristotelian philosophy in ecclesial teachings, and some of Thomas's own propositions were condemned by one of the bishops. He was rehabilitated not long thereafter as the tide swung toward reception of Aristotle's philosophy as handmaiden to theology, due in no small part to Thomas's output. After

> *Thomas Aquinas's* Summa theologiae *stands as one of the most expansive visions of Christian faith ever written.*

his death in 1274, he was officially canonized as saint in 1323, renowned as the "Angelic Doctor" in the mid-fifteenth century, and proclaimed "Doctor of the Church" by Pope Pius V in 1567.

Thomas's great work, the *Summa theologiae*, was written in the last few years before his death and is still being read and studied today. The book is divided into three parts and organized according to over four hundred questions. Each of the questions, reflecting the method of disputation or academic debate prominent in the universities of the mid-thirteenth century, begins with a thesis on the topic at hand, enumerates objections to such, and identifies an additional contrary perspective. Thomas then presents his own constructive response and concludes with replies to remaining objections. More impressive than his approach, however, is the expansiveness of Thomas's theological vision. His work covers the full spectrum of theological questions: about God, creation, angels, divine providence and government, human nature, law and grace, faith-hope-love, the life of discipleship, the incarnation and Christ, the church and its sacraments, resurrection and the last things, and the like. Each of these themes more or less extensively engages in the theological academy of his time. Thomas inquires into historical positions and explores logical and rational responses. Throughout, Thomas reconsiders Christian beliefs in light of the Aristotelian philosophy, although the former is not a slave to the latter in any naive sense. He regularly cites other authorities, especially the church fathers, but is not hesitant to point out when he believes the philosopher is either misguided or inadequate on any specific point. In sum, Thomas provides a foundational reconsideration of the church's teachings by using the Aristotelian ideas that were being explored in the medieval university of his day.

The *Summa theologiae* thus appears as a climactic restatement of Christian doctrine almost a millennium after the establishment of its creedal confessions in the early fourth century. It has shown itself also resilient as an authoritative summation of Christian teaching in the eight and a half centuries since. Particularly after being officially recommended as relevant for the modern world by Pope Leo XIII in his *Æterni Patris*, published in 1879, Thomas's work continues to be studied by Roman Catholic novitiates, ordinands, and scholars. Hence Catholic thinkers and theologians who might be attracted to alternative philosophical systems still cannot avoid dealing with the Thomistic tradition. Even non-Catholic theologians who do not revere Thomas in the same way also have to confront the Angelic Doctor's ideas if they want to engage the broad spectrum of Catholic theological scholarship.

Yet if Thomas was methodologically rigorous, theologically expansive, and dogmatically brilliant, our so-called dumb ox was also known, after attending midday Mass at one point in the last few months of his life, to famously acknowledge to his confidant: "All that I have written seems like straw to me!" This might have been symptomatic of Thomas's suffering from a mental breakdown after years of continuous labor, and it may also have reflected a kind of repudiation of his efforts. Yet Thomas was, not exceptional for his time, also a sort of mystic who in his theological writings regularly granted that human reason and language can only take us so far, and that faith and devotion have their roles to play even in the Christian life of the mind. In the latter perspective, we can appreciate Thomas's recognition that his life's achievements amounted to naught when measured against what may have been a vision into the divine mysteries facilitated by experience of the Eucharist that day.

Young theologians today can find encouragement from Thomas's example along at least three lines. First, we might get off to a relatively slow start, but the work of a theologian gains traction when, as with Thomas, our curiosity compels us, and our inquisitive temperament is acted upon. Even if we may have flunked our first college course, our "dumb ox" friend shows that we can bloom later in life, theologically too, especially if we keep asking questions. Second, for those aspiring to the professional theological vocation, we might want to study further Thomas's life, his work, and his scholarship. We do not have to be Roman Catholics to appreciate how Thomas shows the way forward for those desiring to serve the church and engage the university or the pressing questions of our era. Last but not least, Thomas's admission at the end of his life that his theological reflections were "like straw" ought to be received by ambitious theologians as an admonition toward humility. None of us, no matter how accomplished, can hope to be exhaustively and entirely knowledgeable in things theological. Thomas's assessment puts all of us on the same plane. As prolific (or not) or distinguished (or not), our theological articulations pale when compared with the glories of God that each one of us has experienced. This does not mean that we cannot or should not try to say something, even if "now we see in a mirror, dimly" (1 Cor. 13:12a).

John Wesley as Pastoral and Practical Theologian

John (1703–91) was the fifteenth of nineteen children born to Samuel (1662–1735) and Susanna (1669–1742) Wesley, and he and his younger brother Charles (1707–88) were instrumental in launching what came to be known as the Methodist movement in eighteenth-century England. Both were ordained as clerics in the Church of England and, as college instructors or teachers at Oxford University, founded a "Holy Club" in order to pursue and practice a devout Christian life amid what they considered to be the lackadaisical spiritual climate of their colleges and associated parishes. Still, over the course of the 1730s, through a season of missionary and evangelistic work in Georgia of the Americas that did not end on a high note, and after being introduced to Moravian pietists there and then again upon his return to London, John fell into depression and yearned for renewal in his spirit. On May 24, 1738, at a meeting with fellow Moravian believers on Aldersgate Street, he had his notorious "heart strangely warmed" experience, which revitalized his personal life and reignited his ministry.

Over the rest of his life, it is estimated that Wesley preached over 40,000 sermons and traveled, on horseback usually, over 250,000 miles across England. Although not neglecting to invite sinners to repentance, his message was motivated by his desire, widely acclaimed, "to spread scriptural holiness over the land." Wesley perceived that the dominant Calvinist theology in the Church of England during this time emphasized salvation as a matter of divine election and preservation, thus minimizing human response and perseverance. His adapting then the emphasis on human cooperation (promoted by other theologians) did not lead to abandonment of the theme of God's enablement. Instead, for Wesley, God's prevenient grace elicited human reply, meaning that the Holy Spirit precedes, goes before us, and makes possible our responses. In that sense, divine salvation works itself out in the sanctification of human hearts, the transformation of human lives, and the perfection in love of human actions and behaviors.

Needless to say, Wesley was not a systematic thinker or writer like Thomas Aquinas. However, he wrote out many of his sermons and produced notes and commentary on the entire Bible. As such, he regularly reiterated that he was a "man of one book," the Bible. In addition, he authored hundreds of occasional pieces, oftentimes adapting and editing the works of others in and for his various publications. Having attracted a large following because of his preaching activities, he felt constrained to address certain theological disputes of his day. He often polemicized against Calvinist teachings even though he was famous for designating his own position to be "within a hair's breadth from Calvinism." One of Wesley's most important works, *A Plain Account of Christian Perfection*, clarified misunderstandings that had arisen. The basic contours of his views about sanctification were that Jesus' disciples were called to be holy as the Father in heaven was holy, that they were incapable of attaining such holiness apart from the sanctifying work of the Holy Spirit, and that the Spirit's eradication of the sinful nature would root out the desire to sin and their associated sins of commission. Wesley did recognize that human finitude and frailty would involve us in ongoing sins of omission (unintended acts with consequences that fall short of the ideally purified life). Later generations of Methodist and Wesleyan theologians would debate over whether his account of Christian perfection involved a second divine gift of grace, after regeneration, that produced a work of entire sanctification in human hearts and lives.

> *Wesley embodies theology's call to respond to the needs of everyday life.*

In the end, Wesley was a practical theologian whose writings were motivated by the need to bring clarity to laypersons in the church. His was a religiosity of the heart, confirmed in and through his Aldersgate experience, and expected as normative for all who embraced the biblical message and promises. Yet Wesley's experientialism, unfolding as it did during an era when the Church of England was suspicious about all forms of what was considered enthusiastic or subjective fanaticism, was tempered with his own form of apologetic argument. Wesley was concerned not just about the feelings of the heart but also about the justifications of the mind. In this, his experiential— or experimental, as it was said on occasion at that time—religion was also consistent with his empirical bent. His *Compendium of Natural Philosophy*, also titled *A Survey of the Wisdom of God in Creation*, reflects Wesley the empiricist at work, in the wake of the growing scientific methods emergent from the seventeenth century, although in ways adapted for pastoral purposes. Last but not least, as a preacher and pastoral theologian Wesley was first and foremost a biblicist, although one steeped in both Latin (Western) and Eastern theological traditions of the church.

In short, Wesley the practical and pastoral theologian was rooted in Scripture, oriented by tradition, guided by reason, and empowered by experience, with the Bible being the foundation and capstone. Wesleyan scholars in more recent times have dubbed this fourfold theological orientation around Scripture, tradition, reason, and experience as the *Wesleyan quadrilateral*. This was itself an expansion on the *Anglican triad* of Scripture-tradition-reason that became prominent conceptually in the later nineteenth century. As a faithful member of his church, it might be argued that Wesley the pastor and preacher imbibed the Anglican triad of his day, even before it had been labeled as such. He did add an experiential and empirical direction, but in ways consistent with Anglican sensibilities.

Before commenting further on the Wesleyan quadrilateral and its contribution to the structure of this book, let us take stock of how Wesley might encourage us as young and aspiring theologians. Most of us probably never envisioned serving God as a theologian (I did not in my early days in college) but have yearned to give our lives for the sake of the church and its ministry to and mission for the world. For us, Wesley is a stark reminder that such faithful service for the reign of God is deeply theological, even if we now see this in sermons, Bible studies, and occasional pieces that address contemporary questions rather than in scholarly treatises. As important, even if he was not a professional theologian like Thomas Aquinas, Wesley's life and ministry show us that rationality, pietism, and service—the head, heart, and hands—all belong together and that theology is too important to be avoided. We cannot hope to serve God with all our hearts and hands if we neglect our minds. As Jesus himself urges, "You shall love the Lord your God with all your heart, and with all your soul, and with all your strength, and with all your mind; and your neighbor as yourself" (Luke 10:27).

You and I as Those Who Love God and Want to Know and Serve God

There are any number of figures and names in the history of Christianity that we could have considered in order to inspire our imaginative capacities as those new to theology. Perhaps later, when we look at context and location, we will see that ethnicity, sexuality, and gender matter in ways beyond that portrayed in the preceding profiles. Or we might see that tradition, reason, and experience are abstract concepts masking concrete historical and social realities that inevitably impact our theological paths. As such, our very brief presentations of Macrina, Thomas, and Wesley are merely prompts to jump-start our theological work. There is much more that has been and can be said about each one, even as others in the Christian tradition will inspire our expectations differently as well. Consider the rest of this book an elaboration of theological possibilities implicit in our three prototypes.

Our biographical treks also brought to the fore the Wesleyan quadrilateral that highlights four sources of theological reflection. We have already noted that this was derived from the addition of experience to the Anglican triad of Scripture, tradition, and reason. As with any concept, the quadrilateral is presented merely as a helpful construct. It is neither that other constructs are nonexistent nor that they are unhelpful. But even if there are all kinds of ways to talk about the sources of theology, I think taking up the issues with the help of the quadrilateral provides greater latitude than other alternatives without endlessly multiplying our possibilities. Further, and this is of crucial note, each side (metaphorically speaking) of the quadrilateral is connected to others, and as will be clear in the following, all are interrelated. As a Pentecostal, I am a descendent of the Wesleyan Holiness movement in nineteenth-century America. From this perspective, I will suggest how we can give Scripture high priority even while acknowledging that our reading of Scripture is informed by tradition, reason, and experience.

The first part of this book will therefore proceed according to this quadrilateral frame. Its four chapters (1–4) will move from Scripture to tradition to reason to experience, in each case noting the interdependence of these four sources of theology. Also, in each case we shall show how Christian theologians draw upon these sources in, through, and by the Holy Spirit. This is a bit different from deciphering what theologians have said or might say about the Holy Spirit. Macrina did not say much explicitly about the Spirit; Thomas and Wesley said relatively much more. Yet we shall observe that scriptural interpretation occurs as led by the Spirit in some sense, and that theological traditions can be understood and received as conversation carried by the Spirit. Religious and spiritual encounter, not to mention experience in general, are facilitated by the animation and breath of the Spirit. As such, we shall argue that all theological work is enabled by the Spirit because it is the Spirit that empowers us to draw from Scripture, tradition, reason, and experience for theologically reflective purposes. Understanding the sources of theology is a huge first step for young theologians.

Yet as we also saw above, theological efforts emerge in particular times and places, to address specific purposes. Macrina's theological musings were forged out of conversation with her brother, amid the anxious circumstances of confrontation with death. Thomas's systematically laid out ruminations were also surely incited by questions generated from Aristotelian philosophy, not to mention other developments like the Crusades and the encounter of the medieval church with Islam. And Wesley's sermons and occasional pieces were stimulated by his pastoral practice and concerns. In other words,

> *Theology is part and parcel of what it means to be a Christian.*

theology arises not in a vacuum but amid the hustle and bustle of historical life, including its demands and opportunities.

Part II of this book shifts from the sources of theology to the practices of theologizing. We will look at three contexts: the personal (how theology is related to our individual lives); the ecclesial (how theology is situated within and informs our communal lives, activities, and realities, especially in the community known as *church*); and the educational (how to write and do theology within the context of a class that might have assigned you this book as a text, for instance). The discussion in these three chapters (5–7) will reflect how our theological efforts in each of these contexts are, or can also be, expressions of our life in the Spirit. We will conclude this book with a more extended and substantive discussion of what it means to be theological practitioners in the Spirit and how that suggests that Christian theologians might also be nothing less than Trinitarian theologians (chap. 8).

This book focuses on the work of the Spirit in theology precisely in order to invite readers to think about doing theology as part and parcel of what it means to be a Christian, which is to be filled with the Spirit of Jesus in order to love God and neighbor. Becoming a theologian initially, and then becoming a better and better theologian from then on for the rest of our lives, is interwoven with our Christian discipleship in the Spirit. The study of theology does not ever need to cease, whether we do so formally through theological education or merely wish, as fully as possible, to engage with life as people of Christian faith seeking deeper understanding. Even in the latter case, how we live as believers will involve theological consideration. This book invites followers of Jesus to embrace their theological identity and vocation in order to love God more and better. Welcome to such life in the Spirit that empowers rather than marginalizes the life of the mind.

Discussion Questions

1. What do your tradition and experience tell you about women as theological role models? Who are the women from your family or church who might serve as such examples for young theologians?
2. Although you might not have been called a "dumb ox" before, what are some weaknesses of which you are aware about your own life? How do

you think God might be able to turn these perceived weaknesses into strengths for your theological pilgrimage?

3. Do you relate to Wesley, who was a doer rather than a bookish "nerd"? Can you anticipate how your practicality can nevertheless be part and parcel of a theological vocation?

4. Can you think of other sources of theology beyond Scripture, tradition, reason, and experience? Or what about other contexts of theological reflection beyond the personal and the ecclesial, or after you are finished with this class?

For Further Reading

Chesterton, G. K. *Saint Thomas Aquinas: "The Dumb Ox."* New York: Sheed & Ward, 1956.

Gregory of Nyssa. *The Life of Saint Macrina*. Translated by Kevin Corrigan. Yonkers, NY: Peregrina Publishing, 2001.

Grenz, Stanley J., and Roger E. Olson. *Who Needs Theology? An Invitation to the Study of God*. Downers Grove: InterVarsity Press, 1996.

Kapic, Kelly M. *A Little Book for New Theologians: Why and How to Study Theology*. Downers Grove: IVP Academic, 2014.

Kerr, Fergus. *Thomas Aquinas: A Very Short Introduction*. Oxford: Oxford University Press, 2009.

Luck, Donald. *Why Study Theology?* St. Louis: Chalice Press, 1999.

Parratt, John. *A Guide to Doing Theology*. Minneapolis: Fortress Press, 2015.

Silva, Anna. *Macrina the Younger: Philosopher of God*. Turnhout, Belgium: Brepols, 2008.

Stone, Howard W., and James O. Duke. *How to Think Theologically*. 3rd ed. Minneapolis: Fortress Press, 2013.

Thompson, Ross. *Is There an Anglican Way? Scripture, Church, and Reason: New Approaches to an Old Triad*. London: Darton, Longman & Todd, 1997.

Thorsen, Donald A. D. *The Wesleyan Quadrilateral: Scripture, Tradition, Reason, and Experience as a Model of Evangelical Theology*. Grand Rapids: Zondervan, 1990.

Tyson, John R. *The Way of the Wesleys: A Short Introduction*. Grand Rapids: Wm. B. Eerdmans Publishing Co., 2014.

Wicks, Jared, SJ. *Doing Theology*. New York: Paulist Press, 2009.

Yong, Amos. *Spirit-Word-Community: Theological Hermeneutics in Trinitarian Perspective*. Eugene, OR: Wipf & Stock, 2002.

PART I

The Sources of Theology

1

Scripture

The Word and Breath of God

The Bible is indisputably central to Christian life and faith. If you were raised in church, you certainly have heard many sermons or homilies from the Bible, and if you were introduced to Christianity later in life, you have come also to realize how important this book is to Christians. In this chapter, we will see how the Bible is not only the most important resource for theology but also suggest how it can or should be used in theological reflection.

Our discussion will revolve around three sets of interpretive methods usually brought to reading the Bible. The first looks at the world *behind* the text (historical and critical approaches). The second focuses on the world *of* the text (literary and narrative approaches). The third connects to the world *in front of* the text (pragmatic and performative approaches). We shall see that as each moment is interwoven with the others, theological interpretation presumes their togetherness. We will then conclude by considering, in a very preliminary way, how we can and should listen to the Holy Spirit speaking through these scriptural moments to the church (and its members) to empower Christian practice and belief (theology) in every age and every situation.

Remember that our use of the Wesleyan quadrilateral construct means that we see Scripture to be interlinked with tradition, reason, and experience, all as theological resources. This means that our discussion of Scripture in this chapter anticipates and, in many respects, presumes what is said in the rest of part I of this book. While in the abstract we might be able to discuss Scripture apart from how it is encountered and engaged in real life, given our own commitments to its authoritative character for Christian life and faith, we will attempt to revere Scripture on its own terms as much as possible. But we will signal ahead, as needed, to indicate that our approach is perhaps more circular than linear across the four chapters of this first part of the book.

1.1. Behind the Text

What is the world behind the text, and why is it important? This has to do partly with how to understand the references of the biblical message. The Bible tells stories—of Israel, its leaders, or the apostles and others—and these stories contribute to one overarching story of God's relationship with the world. The word "Christian" derives from the person of Jesus Christ, who is presented in the Gospels as the Logos or Word of God, who "became flesh and lived among us" (John 1:14a). The good news rests on this historical person: "We declare to you what was from the beginning, what we have heard, what we have seen with our eyes, what we have looked at and touched with our hands, concerning the word of life" (1 John 1:1). In short, while skeptics might think that these stories are made up, Christian faith rests on their having happened in some respect as accounted for in the pages of the Bible. This is not to say that every biblical story happened exactly as it is written in the text. It is to say that study of the world behind the text is important, both because of the historicity of Christian faith and in order to understand the nature of what happened in relationship to how such stories are told across the Scriptures.

There are at least three kinds of "tools" or methodologies, each overlapping in some way, that we can deploy when attempting to grasp this world behind the text. The first, *the historical method*, attempts to understand the text in relationship to what happened. Here confirming evidences are sought for what is presented in the biblical narratives from nonbiblical sources. Part of the goal here is to determine, according to more-or-less established historical methods, what happened. Much of this relies on some form of what is called analogical thinking, which is the equivalence, more or less, between what we read and our own experience. Thus we might be more inclined to believe a text's account of what happened if we ourselves have experienced something like what the text describes. Or we might be disinclined to accept such claims if they seem too far removed from our own sense of reality. Yet the challenge of the biblical narratives is that they often involve more or less fantastic events and developments. Jesus' resurrection from the dead is a prime example. Hence historical methods can never provide absolute assurance. At some level, we approach the Bible in faith, and it might be that a dynamic personal encounter with God (to be explored in chap. 5) makes it possible for us to accept, tentatively at least, what the Bible appears to say despite its less-than-easy believability.

A second and related approach is *historical and grammatical analysis*. This is focused on how to understand what authors are communicating through their texts against the background of their historical contexts. Texts are produced by an author, or a group of authors, in certain historical periods of time, perhaps slightly or even quite removed from the time of the events that are being described. For instance, the book of Joel seems to be about a plague of locusts that may have happened as early as the late ninth century BCE. But the prophecy may have been written a few hundred years later, even after the exile to Babylon in the sixth

> *Historical context—what we can know about human life and the events that shaped it—is central to understanding the world behind the text.*

century. Alternatively, we might not know exactly when Joel was written, but perhaps certain grammatical clues are suggestive. The style of writing might also help us discern whether it was written closer to or much later than the events purported therein. If authors of texts can be determined with greater rather than lesser certainty, we know who these persons were, what their historical context was like, how their language was used in that time, and why they may have chosen to produce the text that bears their name. Such knowledge can enable further our comprehension of what they have written. In many cases, however, we may not know who the authors are, so we have to decipher from the text what might have motivated its writing. Further, internal textual or grammatical cues combined with external witnesses (e.g., other texts that provide confirming accounts) may enable us to determine approximately when a text may have been written, and this gives us some perspective so we can better understand its historical context. From a Christian perspective, however, we might say that all texts, regardless of who they are from and when they were produced, are divinely authorized by the Spirit of God. This is "because no prophecy ever came by human will, but men and women moved by the Holy Spirit spoke from God" (2 Pet. 1:21). "Prophecy" here is a more generic reference to the Scriptures of the Old Testament and hence applicable to the Bible more broadly.

This leads us to *canonical criticism*, the method of considering Scripture as one book or canon. Historically, then, the world behind the text involves (1) the world described by the text, (2) the world of the author/s that produced such texts, and (3) the world of developments that led to the collection of such texts into certain configurations that eventually resulted in what we call the Bible. This last aspect of the world behind the text is important for at least two reasons. First, if we can comprehend why a text was eventually included in the scriptural canon, we can better realize how it was viewed as authoritative for others and hence also for ourselves (in contrast to other texts that may not have been canonized). Second, if we can appreciate how these texts were understood in relationship to each other, for instance in their ordered sequence rather than other possible arrangements, we can better follow how others have seen the progression of the big story of God's relationship with the world amid the many little stories that contribute to that narrative. In short, a canonical perspective helps us both to grasp how Jewish and Christian reading communities came to accept texts as divinely communicative and to connect the dots across the two sections of Scripture.

1.2. The World of the Text

Considerations of Scripture as canon lead us into the text of the Bible itself. Here, canonicity foregrounds one of the Bible's major interpretive principles: that we interpret Scripture in part by Scripture. Earlier parts of Scripture (e.g., in the Old Testament) may be understood afresh in light of later portions (e.g., in the New Testament), even as readings of the latter are also in part shaped by our understandings of the former. Or one Gospel account could be supplemented by the others, although the integrity of each writer and text ought to be respected, and apparent discrepancies ought not to be too quickly harmonized just in order to eliminate our uncomfortable dissonance.

> *Intertextuality = how scriptural writers directly quote or more indirectly allude to other biblical texts.*

Some scholars discuss canonical interpretation in terms of intertextuality. This refers not just to reading one part of the Bible in relationship to the other parts but to how scriptural writers directly quote or more indirectly allude to other biblical texts. The author of the Hebrews, for instance, quotes one of the psalms (95:7–11), the group of which are elsewhere in the New Testament understood to be of Davidic authorship. But in this case, Hebrews describes such as being words of the Holy Spirit (Heb. 3:7–11). Such an ascription invites a consideration of this segment of the Letter to the Hebrews in dialogue with this psalmic passage in particular, and with the traditions of Israel's wilderness wandering in prior portions of the Old Testament that have fed this psalmic text. There are intertextual echoes all over the canon. Earlier Old Testament texts appear in later Old Testament (also known as the Hebrew Bible) writings. In the New Testament, there are intertextual connections between various portions of the Christian writings as well.

Intertextual criticism leads in one direction toward literary criticism. The key here is attending to the various genres across the Bible and observing how each one functions in accordance with how such genres were meant to communicate in ancient times. The creation narratives operate less as a modern historical treatise and more like a mythic account of the world in relationship to God. In contrast to other ancient Near Eastern cosmogonies (creation myths or stories), however, the world in Genesis is dependent on a personal God rather than emanating from impersonal divine forces. Similarly, the historical books of the Old Testament are sometimes inconsistent from the perspective of those wanting to know what exactly happened. Did Yahweh (the Hebrew name for God) incite David to take the census (2 Sam. 24:1–2) or did Satan ("an adversary," 1 Chr. 21:1 NET)? There are different time periods and circumstances behind these narratives. Samuel is a kind of prophetic and historical book, while Chronicles is a scribal tradition that seeks a new understanding of Israel's fortunes in light of the Babylonian exile. Attention here to the world behind the text can therefore be suggestive of why these so-called accounts are different from modern histories that seek only to record what exactly happened. Instead, they are of a more theological type that understands historical events, in all their complexity, in relationship to transcendent (good or not too good, in this case) realities.

The point is that the Bible is constituted by different types of literature from the ancient world: (1) historical accounts that have theological dimensions (which modern histories do not have), (2) poetry, (3) prophecies, (4) lamentations, (5) letters (epistles), (6) gospels (unique in the ancient world), and so forth. Each must be understood against its historical setting but also following the interpretive guidelines relative to such literary forms. Poetic texts must be respected as affective and evocative in ways less relevant to more didactic epistolary segments of the canon, for instance. Prophetic texts, in contrast, presume an interactivity between God and the world. If not granted, that will inhibit any real engagement with these writings.

> *The basic teachings of Scripture exist, not as abstract propositions, but within stories that are enveloped by the story.*

Yet in the main, the various genres exist within and are located across the overarching narrative of the scriptural canon that for Jews persists from Genesis through Malachi and for Christians extends through Revelation, or the Apocalypse. As such, there is a kind of biblical metanarrative, or overarching story, that is all-embracing of the various textual genres and other literary elements. In the twenty-first century, there is suspicion in some quarters of metanarratives as being presumptuous since human beings only have finite perspective. Yet it is also undeniable that some kind of big picture precedes and informs all understanding. It is therefore important to acknowledge that our overall assumptions are constantly changing and shifting in response to our experience. As such, Scripture is best approached narratively: as one dramatic chronicle of God as Creator and Redeemer. Yet this one account is punctuated by many different, not always cohesive, stories (or "histories," keeping in mind the differences between ancient and modern notions of this term), whether that of Abraham, Moses, David, Jesus, the apostles, and the like.

In any case, the basic teachings of Scripture exist not as abstract propositions but as situated within stories that are enveloped by *the* story. It is not that the Bible contains no theological or doctrinal teachings, but that such claims and statements are best received within the historical and canonical contexts within which they have been communicated. "Absolute truths" that are presented as fairly straightforward philosophical or metaphysical propositions are relatively absent within the scriptural narrative. This does not mean that a biblically informed theology cannot eventually make so-called universal claims. It is to say that any such assertions *arise* from Scripture, but are not the content of Scripture itself: the Bible is primarily telling stories rather than uttering theological or philosophical propositions.

To be sure, stories have affective and emotive potency, and this means that they ought to be critically assessed so that we don't just twist these narratives to say what any of us might want them to say. In a sense, the whole first part of this book is intended to provide a range of tools to enable such sober analysis and reception. However, criticism here is in the service of faith, a kind of faith-in-the-biblical-God-seeking-understanding, as it were. For the moment, however, we have already begun to see that literary and narrative interpretations exist not by themselves, but as approaches also related to and informed by historical, grammatical, and canonical hermeneutics.

1.3. In Front of the Text

Thus far we have looked at how the world *behind the text* refers to the historical circumstances that are related in the text and led to the generation of the text and its canonization. We have also seen how the world *of the text* concerns its genres and cohesiveness. Now we turn to examine how the world *in front of the text* has to do with its *reception history*, its *history of effects*, and related developments. Strictly understood, reception history concerns how a text has been received, how it was understood, interpreted, and debated by later readers. History of effects, or effective history, on the other hand, includes additionally how a text may have had real-life impact, for instance, in informing the practices of readers or shaping ecclesial or extra-ecclesial policies and interactions for good or ill. For instance, both slaveholders and abolitionists used the Bible to justify their position in the nineteenth century. To be sure, historical causation never depends on just one variable, even one so important as its scriptural warrants, so the history of effects of sacred texts, the Bible included, involves many factors.

Nevertheless, observe that the history of scriptural interpretation, part of its reception and effective history, continues to affect the way later generations read and engage with the Bible. Even if readers in general and young theologians more particularly are not aware of such historical developments, each of us approaches the Bible informed by our own histories, which to greater or lesser

> *The "world in front of the text" = what Scripture has meant to its readers.*

degrees include listening to sermons, participating in Bible studies, or being privy to this or that conversation about the Bible. And preachers, Bible study leaders, or laypeople at large have also been influenced by the Bible's reception and effective history, whether because they have attended seminaries, had other formal theological or educational training, or simply heard sermons or participated in Bible studies going back years, even decades. Thus the world in front of the text, in this case the reception and effective histories of the Scriptures, shape how every generation of readers and thinkers interacts with the Bible.

If some might worry that these histories are impositions on the way in which the Bible ought to be read, notice that Scripture itself invites readers to experience its claims. "O taste and see that the LORD is good" (Ps. 34:8a), the psalmist bids. On the other hand, late in the apostolic period, the author of the Letter to Timothy describes the purpose of Scripture in this way: "From childhood you have known the sacred writings that are able to instruct you for salvation through faith in Christ Jesus. All scripture is inspired by God and is useful for teaching, for reproof, for correction, and for training in righteousness, so that everyone who belongs to God may be proficient, equipped for every good work" (2 Tim. 3:15–17). Scripture instructs to save, and within this overarching frame, it teaches, reproves, corrects, and purifies. In short, the Bible enables and inspires proficiency in good works.

There is then a sense, adhering to the canonical and intertextual principles, that this Timothean text summons all Christians to be taught, admonished, and finally saved and sanctified in and through interaction with the Bible. From this perspective, other scriptural cues become clear. For instance, the author of the Fourth Gospel concludes by putting plainly the purpose for his writing: "Now Jesus did many other signs in the presence of his disciples, which are not written in this book. But these are written so that you may come to believe that Jesus is the Messiah, the Son of God, and that through believing you may have life in his name" (John 20:30–31). We might read the Gospel of John for many different reasons and even learn many other things. But whether we accept it or not, we cannot and should not deny that he wrote in order that we might believe in Jesus and receive the eternal life (mentioned repeatedly in John) that comes through him. Hence, especially because it is difficult to determine what it means to believe in Jesus and experience eternal life in him, the reception history, including testimonies of contemporaries, to that effect ought to both inform our understanding of this Gospel and shape our own experience of it.

To say that interpreting the Bible needs to include its reception and effective history and that this involves the history of experiences of the text might be a bit worrisome. Yet if we might be rightly uneasy that individual experience could just as much distort as elucidate the Scriptures, let us not forget the role of the Holy Spirit in this process. The Bible itself tutors as such, as in the letters to the seven churches addressed in the book of Revelation: "Let anyone who has an ear listen to what the Spirit is saying to the churches" (Rev. 2:7a; also 2:11a, 17a, 29; 3:6, 13, 22). Hence to listen (or read, in our case) and then to live in light of what we have heard (or read) cannot or should not be dissociated from the Holy Spirit. To be sure, it is sometimes difficult to discern between our being led by the Spirit and our claiming as such. Yet this challenge ought not to lead to a complete dismissal of the Spirit's leading role in effectuating in our lives the realities testified to by Scripture.

Now, those concerned only with the world behind the text might want to limit application of this instruction only to members of the seven churches of Revelation who received the original missive of visions. There is a sense in which we should be careful about collapsing the distances between the world behind and the world in front of the text so that we do not presume that if Judas went and hanged himself (Matt. 27:5; Acts 1:16–18), so also should we! That is why it is important to develop tools to discern how to maintain the respective domains of the worlds behind, within, and in front of the Bible. The rest of the chapters in part I of this book will bring further clarification to these important matters.

1.4. The Spirit of the Text

We have already seen that the Holy Spirit can be understood to have inspired the text to begin with, and in that sense the Spirit links the world behind the text (§1.1) with the world of the text (§1.2). We now realize that the Spirit works also in the world in front of the text (§1.3). Historically, this has been where the role of the Spirit has been most pronounced. The Spirit illuminates the meaning of the text to readers and then applies the text in and through their lives. Some might insist on the distinction between meaning (in the original context) and application (in the readers' context) and this would in effect suggest that the Spirit works in the worlds *of the text* (the meaning as grammatically, literarily, and narratively understood) and *in front of the text* (the application of such meaning). Yet such delineation would be too hard and fast. Rather, bringing them together, it might be said that the Spirit brings the text to life for later readers, communities, and generations. As Paul himself intimated in discussing the old covenant and the written law, "The letter kills, but the Spirit gives life" (2 Cor. 3:6b). I emphasize the role of the Spirit in all three moments: prior to the text, generating the text; in the text's canonization; and in its effective capacity.

Putting it this way reflects pietist and pragmatist sensibilities regarding the Bible. Pietists are among those who insist that the Bible is first and foremost a book that is *for* believers. The Bible builds them up in the faith and in that sense is applicable to their lives of discipleship. Pietists would contend, "Indeed, the word of God is living and active, sharper than any two-edged sword, piercing until it divides soul from spirit, joints from marrow; it is able to judge the thoughts and intentions of the heart" (Heb. 4:12). Some pietists have been what in earlier times were called primitivists and restorationists. These were heirs of the Renaissance (and then Reformation) retrieval of ancient texts who focused on a recovery of the apostolic way of life as recorded in the pages of the New Testament. Contemporary pietists are far from the only Christians who embrace the active role of the Bible in their lives. Most theological or confessional interpreters of Scripture today would be likely to accept that Scripture invites inhabitation and participation. The difference is that pietists have been more likely historically and still also in the present to invoke the Spirit devotionally and thereby experience Scripture's power and reality.

Pragmatists might refer to a philosophical movement, but the context of this discussion involves also the views of those who claim that the meaning of any text includes its effects. For instance, how we might understand God's nature and character is less a propositional matter and more related to the qualities manifest in the lives of those committed to that Deity. So, what it means to say that "God is love" is clarified by the love manifest in the lives of those making this claim. Therefore the effects of any text, whether intentionally enacted by readers because they believe such to be textually demanded or unintentionally performed, tell us about that text's meaning and significance. (Meaning and significance are technically distinct in the broader hermeneutical literature, but not for pragmatists.) So if no one who says "God is love" shows love, then it is difficult to comprehend what this claim is asserting. In short, the worlds behind, within, and in front of the text are interconnected. In this sense, the meaning and significance of a text in its original context are related to pragmatic applications in their contexts, and vice versa.

One scriptural example might be helpful to see how pietism and pragmatism are intertwined in the effects of Scripture. On the Day of Pentecost, Luke, the author of the book of Acts, records Peter preaching from the prophet Joel to explain the developments to the crowd concerning the outpouring of the Holy Spirit (Acts 2:14–21; cf. Joel 2:28–32). There are many worlds *behind* the text in this case that are not quite clear-cut:

1. Joel's *world* behind Joel's *text* (historically murky as indicated in §1.1 above), because the book of Joel was probably written some considerable period of time after the prophet's life)
2. Joel's text *behind Peter's preaching*
3. Joel's text in Peter's preaching *behind Luke's text*
4. Joel's text in Peter's preaching as recorded in Luke's text *behind the reception of Luke's text* (which history is ongoing!)
5. and so on

There are similarly multiple textual worlds here: of Joel's and of Luke's, most clearly. And there are also many worlds *in front of the text*: the world in front of Joel's text, and that in front of Luke's. As we can see, how Luke is understood depends on how Peter read Joel and how Joel ought to be comprehended on his own terms and in relationship to the prophetic literature with which it is associated (the Book of the Twelve). Yet something further is just as important for our pragmatist inclinations: how Joel is understood is now influenced by Peter's reception and by Luke's account and the latter's reception and effective history. We understand better if we also have received the Holy Spirit as the text seems to describe than if we had no such experiences. To summarize: the meaning of any text is neither fully determined nor complete: its sense is subject to its ongoing application in human hearts (the pietist emphasis) and lives (the pragmatist focus).

From a Christian perspective, I suggest that this can be understood *pentecostally*, in relationship to the giving of the Holy Spirit at what the Bible describes as the Pentecost event (Acts 2). As a contemporary pentecostal Christian, I suggest that all Christian reading and understanding of the Bible is *after* Pentecost, meaning enabled by the Holy Spirit. In this connection, not only does the Spirit bring about intellectual cognition of the words of the Bible: it also enables the realization of these words in relation to the salvation and sanctification that God intends for us. Ours is thereby a growing understanding of Scripture, facilitated by the Holy Spirit, who actualizes the message of the Bible afresh in our lives and in the new circumstances of our world. How this happens will be further unveiled in the rest of this book.

Discussion Questions

1. Why is the world *behind the text* important for our reading the Bible? In what ways does understanding of that world help to provide guidelines for how we might interpret the message of Scripture?
2. Can you provide in a few sentences the overarching dramatic narrative of the Bible? Might you be able to indicate how some of its various texts contribute to that account?
3. What are some reasons the Bible and its various texts give for their being written? How effective have these been or how have these been actualized or realized by individuals or the church more generally since Bible times?
4. Can you summarize what the Bible teaches with regard to the role of the Holy Spirit *before, within,* and *in front of* the Scriptures? How, if at all, is the Holy Spirit present in your own interaction with the Bible?

For Further Reading

Archer, Kenneth J. *A Pentecostal Hermeneutic for the Twenty-First Century: Spirit, Scripture, and Community.* Journal of Pentecostal Theology Supplement 28. New York: Bloomsbury / T&T Clark, 2004.

Brown, Jeannine. *Scripture as Communication: Introducing Biblical Hermeneutics.* Grand Rapids: Baker Academic, 2007.

Fee, Gordon D., and Douglas Stuart. *How to Read the Bible for All Its Worth.* 4th ed. Grand Rapids: Zondervan, 2014.

Gorman, Michael J. *Elements of Biblical Exegesis: A Basic Guide for Students and Ministers.* Rev. ed. Grand Rapids: Baker Academic, 2008.

Keener, Craig S. *Spirit Hermeneutics: Reading Scripture in the Light of Pentecost.* Grand Rapids: Wm. B. Eerdmans Publishing Co., 2016.

Noel, Bradley Truman. *Pentecostal and Postmodern Hermeneutics: Comparisons and Contemporary Impact.* Eugene, OR: Wipf & Stock, 2010.

Osborne, Grant. *The Hermeneutical Spiral: A Comprehensive Introduction to Biblical Interpretation.* Downers Grove, IL: InterVarsity Press, 1991.

Smith, James K. A. *The Fall of Interpretation: Philosophical Foundations for a Creational Hermeneutic.* 2nd ed. Grand Rapids: Baker Academic, 2012.

Spawn, Kevin L., and Archie T. Wright, eds. *Spirit and Scripture: Exploring a Pneumatic Hermeneutic*. New York: Bloomsbury / T&T Clark, 2013.

Tate, W. Randolph. *Biblical Interpretation: An Integrated Approach*. Rev. ed. Peabody, MA: Hendrickson Publishers, 1997.

Thiselton, Anthony. *New Horizons in Hermeneutics*. Grand Rapids: Zondervan, 1992.

Yong, Amos. *The Hermeneutical Spirit: Theological Interpretation and the Scriptural Imagination for the Third Christian Millennium*. Eugene, OR: Cascade Books, 2017.

2

Tradition

The Living Body of Christ and the Fellowship
of the Holy Spirit

The Wesleyan quadrilateral, as an extension of the Anglican triad, includes tradition as a secondary theological resource after Scripture. The previous chapter attempted to clarify how the Bible can and should be retrieved for theological purposes. It also suggested, especially in the discussion of reception and effective history, how Scripture and tradition are in that respect continuous. This chapter considers how the scriptural traditions are related to, as well as handed down through, ecclesial and theological traditions. This chapter also explores how both are undergoing fresh reception amid the contemporary global ferment; it also proposes how the Holy Spirit both extends and corrects tradition and in every age brings forth new developments in the church to guide the theologizing process.

The four sections of this chapter move both historically and in a spiral. We begin first with theological tradition especially in the main lines of the Eastern Orthodox and Latin/Roman churches, focusing specifically on the dialectic between formal institutions on the one hand, and charisma (or charismatic leadership) on the other. We move then to Protestant churches and their heirs, where we will discuss especially the diversity of doctrinal and theological developments in these movements. The third section on world Christianity outside the Euro-American orbit interfaces with both Western and Eastern theological traditions (since the lines between the history of Christianity and the history of Christian mission are no longer as solid) in order to get a sense for how theology has been contextual from its beginnings. The final section will attempt to provide some pentecostal and pneumatological perspective on the role of the Spirit in the traditioned development of theology and doctrine.

As already indicated, our discussion of tradition in this chapter is in some respects arbitrarily excerpted from the other elements of the quadrilateral matrix. The following develops our thinking (see above) about Scripture as theological resource even as we anticipate the discussions on reason and experience in the next two chapters. If we keep in mind that Scripture-tradition-reason-experience are interrelated, then this chapter's considerations ought to have implications both backward and forward. Precisely for these reasons, we must keep the ongoing work of the Holy Spirit ever present in mind, as this chapter hopes also to do.

2.1. Church and Tradition: Charisma and Institution

What is tradition? Albeit difficult to define, it may be best understood by discussing, however briefly, some of the various traditions that constitute Christianity. One dimension of tradition is its conciliar (related to councils) or creedal character. In the history of the church there have been seven ecumenical (universal) church councils, meetings of church bishops and other leaders. The first met at Nicaea in 325 CE, and the last convened in 787 in that same city. These are considered ecumenical in the sense that they involved the whole church, before the division in 1054 that separated the churches of western Europe (which came to be known as Roman Catholicism) from those of eastern Europe (which came to be known as Eastern Orthodoxy). Among the many canons or decisions that these seven councils entered, the most important might be the creeds developed at Nicaea in 325 and Chalcedon in 451. The Nicene Creed was confirmed and slightly elaborated at the Council of Constantinople in 381, combining to define the doctrine of the Trinity. The Constantinopolitan Creed clarified Jesus Christ as one person with both divine and human natures. Hence conciliar traditions involve these confessions or creeds that most, though not all, Christians believe to be binding for the faith and the church's self-understanding.

> *Eastern Christians celebrate tradition through their liturgies, in which the role of the Spirit is central.*

The Eastern Orthodox churches assign particular authority to the theological definitions and creeds developed at the seven ecumenical councils. There is a sense in which Eastern Christians understand their own tradition as the most authentic and encompassing of the faith. Yet apart from these early creeds, most Eastern churches view their theological identity less through formal statements and more through their liturgical practices. Thus, to be

Orthodox involves at least adherence to these ecumenical creeds not only in the confessional sense but also in their liturgical practices. Orthodoxy's "tradition," as they understand it, is manifest in their worship. And given the centrality of the Spirit in the prayers of *epiclesis* (calling forth the Holy Spirit), of invocation, and throughout the various moments of the liturgy, the Orthodox see themselves as fully Trinitarian believers both in name and in practice. Their "tradition" is what it is because of, rather than over and against, the reality of the Holy Spirit in the church.

While the Eastern understandings of tradition about the Spirit are not uncontested (both within and outside Orthodoxy), they highlight how tradition and Spirit have sometimes been construed as contraries in the Roman Catholic West. Even if Orthodox and Catholics do not see tradition as opposed to the authority and even priority of Scripture, there is a more robustly liturgical dimension to tradition in the East that contrasts with the additionally substantive magisterium, or "teaching office," overseeing the doctrines and teachings of the Roman Church: this contrast has developed over the course of the last fifteen hundred years. While the bishops of the Eastern churches continue to meet and make theological decisions, they do not consider those meetings to equal the seven ecumenical councils in authority. The situation is different in Roman Catholicism. Its bishops have continued to gather in ecumenical councils whose theological decrees are considered binding for all Catholics (including those of the most recent, the Second Vatican Council, which met in 1962–65). Roman Catholic councils are complemented in addition by decrees, encyclicals, and other official writings emanating from the Roman administration. Tradition in the Roman Catholic Church therefore has generated an extensive set of documents, all developed institutionally in and through the church's teachings and offices.

There has therefore been a rather long debate, especially in the Latin West, about how the institutional structures of the church can facilitate dynamics that inevitably drive organizational change historically. For the church, this is both a sociological and theological question, so much so that it has been discussed in some quarters as a tension between prophecy and order, or between charisma and institution. If the church is a living organism, metaphorically understood according to the New Testament as the *body of Christ*, then the church is not static but grows and develops. From a pneumatological and Trinitarian perspective, this might be set up as a contest between the charismatic activities of the divine Spirit in and through the church and its members on the one hand, and the institutionalized orders of the *ecclesia* (church) on the other. The former "communion [fellowship] of the Holy Spirit" (2 Cor. 13:13) would contrast with the latter forces of government more interested in preserving the status quo than in adaptation and change.

Unsurprisingly, then, the history of Christianity is fraught with the emergence of charismatic movements, often at the margins, seeking renewal of the whole church. "Prophetic" voices, often challenging "the way things are," are usually vilified by institutional powers that resist giving way to new forms and configurations. To be sure, the church institutional has tried to accommodate renewal movements, for instance by integrating monastic reform groups and assimilating charismatic groups. In that sense, institution and charisma are not finally at odds, even if historically they have often been in tension with one another.

In this short space we cannot hope to provide any comprehensive coverage of Catholic or Orthodox churches, even as later in this chapter we will return to clarify developments of these traditions in the majority world. For the moment, however, note that traditions can function variously for theological purposes, such as by informing us confessionally and creedally, by shaping us liturgically, or by guiding us magisterially, among other means. Regardless, the role of the Spirit persists and ought not to be ignored in our thinking about how we do theology in dialogue with the traditions that constitute our faith.

2.2. The Spirit/s of Protestantism

The Protestant Reformation of the early sixteenth century arose initially as intending to reform the Western Roman Church. Also drawing inspiration from the Renaissance's "return to the classic sources" initiative (§1.4 above), the Reformers' most important methodological decision was to prioritize Scripture as the primary, if not singular, source of theological authority. The Roman Catholic Church believed divine revelation came through the two sources of Scripture and the traditions of the church, but the Reformers held Scripture alone (*sola scriptura*) as the only source for theology. *Sola scriptura* ought not to be taken too literally because it stands alongside other *solae*: grace alone, faith alone, Christ alone, and the glory of God alone. Further,

> *In Protestantism, Scripture is the primary (some would say the only) source of theological authority.*

sola scriptura was part of the Reformation protest to what was perceived as a devaluation of the authority of the Bible or at least its subordination to the ongoing accumulation of tradition (e.g., the magisterium). Some segments of the so-called Radical Reformation were among the first primitivists and restorationists (also §1.4) who insisted that only the apostolic beliefs and practices recorded in the New Testament are authoritative for Christians. These Radical Reformers also minimized, if not dismissed altogether, much of postapostolic creedal, papal, or magisterial additions as nonessential for the church's self-understanding.

The Roman Catholic Church responded with the Council of Trent (1545–63). The council agreed in general that many of the proposed reforms were needed but it also identified tendencies in the *solae* that would lead to further fragmentation of the church for those who followed its path. The Council of Trent worried that Protestants had deprived the Bible of the ecclesial traditions that had heretofore provided at least some guidance for formulating the church's doctrines and official teachings. Without these constraints, as anticipated by Trent, various Protestant movements that followed on the heels of the Reformation, such as the Lutheran and then later the Reformed Christians, developed their own confessions, and later the Anabaptists (of the Radical Reformation) dismissed the role of creeds altogether. The Church of England sought a middle way between Protestant *sola scriptura* and Roman Catholic Scripture-and-tradition (roughly speaking). But by then, numerous other "traditions" had emerged, later called denominations. As discussed in the introduction, Wesley was a faithful member of the Anglican Church and never intended to start another church. Still, Methodism arose instead, and this Wesleyan stream opened up over the next century and a half to numerous other churches (denominations now).

> *Is the pentecostal movement a branch of Protestantism, or does it constitute its own distinct way of being Christian?*

In North America during the nineteenth century, Wesleyan preachers, in their mission to spread the message of scriptural perfection all over the (new) continent, forged a holiness movement and also organized, in due course, multiple churches and denominations. This holiness tributary opened up at the beginning of the twentieth century to a pentecostal revival, centered in Los Angeles (albeit with parallel developments elsewhere), that produced also their own churches and, later, denominations. Within a generation or two, further renewing movements ensued, including charismatic expressions across Protestant denominations and in Roman Catholic and Eastern Orthodox communions. In the last third of the twentieth century, the pentecostal revival had not only spread around the world but had also played a significant role in the recentering of Christianity away from the Euro-American West toward the global South.

There is ongoing debate about the degree to which pentecostal and charismatic renewal movements constitute their own fourth type of Christian tradition, alongside Roman Catholicism, Eastern Orthodoxy, and Protestantism. To some extent, pentecostal-charismatic spirituality is internal to, rather than external from, these historic traditions. From another perspective, the pentecostal-charismatic churches purport to have their own character. It is also the case that pentecostal churches and denominations are historically situated within more conservative Protestant traditions, especially in their pietist manifestations. Thus, when the National Association of Evangelicals was organized in North America in 1942, it included within it some pentecostal denominations, like the Assemblies of God. To be sure, what "evangelical" means remains disputed. Yet the origins of the so-called evangelicalism of today has deep roots in the protest movements that articulated the *solae* in the Reformation period. The result is sometimes confusing since we have very conservative evangelical churches on one side of the spectrum and more established and historic churches on the far other side, separated by deep differences of opinion and practice. The *Evangelische Kirche in Deutschland* (the Evangelical Church in Germany), for example, traces its genealogy to the earliest days of the Reformation, but it is not evangelical in the conservative North American Protestant sense.

> *The tension between institution and charisma persists.*

This means that there are more conservative and more progressive trajectories not just across the Christian tradition considered ecumenically or universally, but also within the churches (Roman Catholicism, for instance), certainly within the Protestant "camp." Reformed or evangelical or pentecostal churches, for instance, all exist across a spectrum. At the same time, within Protestantism, there are developments such as the Joint Declaration on the Doctrine of Justification, agreed to in 1999, that sought to heal the divisions of the Reformation. Those who embrace not just the letter but also the spirit of this document are more likely to see a convergence between traditions going forward. Part of the point is that traditions themselves are constantly adjusting so that their identities today are different tomorrow. Yet many Protestant denominations and churches would retain a non-Catholic, if not anti-Catholic, self-understanding for the foreseeable future. In these cases, the issue is that the tension discussed above between institution (even of Protestant movements) and charisma (the forces open to change) persists. Protest movements, often originating on the prophetic and charismatic margins, eventually also institutionalize and become traditions that in turn resist further transformation. In such traditions the more conservative, by nature and definition, are more cautious about revisions to what is for them a biblically warranted status quo. Those more progressive, alternatively, are just as likely to be innovative for reasons they believe are fundamental to Protestant (e.g., biblical) principles. As such, if it is the work of the Spirit to transform not just human hearts but also ecclesial traditions in anticipation of the coming divine reign, then tradition as a resource for theology remains fundamentally a changing (Spirit-led and inspired, one hopes) concern and reality.

2.3. The Church Catholic as the Fellowship of the Spirit

We now pick up threads from the preceding sections of this discussion to further the task of what it means to do theology in dialogue with the church's traditions in today's world. Although much of our discussion of Catholicism, Orthodoxy, and Protestantism in this chapter has focused on developments in the Western world, there have been Christian presences outside the West even early on during the first millennium. Eastern forms of the Christian tradition were taken by Syrian missionaries across the Silk Road into Central and South Asia even as early as the second century. Then Coptic and other Orthodox missionaries built on the legacy of the Ethiopian eunuch in the Acts narrative (8:26–40) to develop Orthodox communities on the eastern seaboard of Africa not long thereafter. Going in the other direction across the Atlantic, Roman Catholic missionaries evangelized the "new world" and have thoroughly enculturated the Catholic tradition across the Central and South Americas over the last half millennium. Directly south of the Mediterranean, in the meanwhile, vibrant forms of early Christian faith existed during the first five hundred years after Christ, even as Africa has become increasingly Christianized since the colonial period. Much of Christianity across Asia, Africa, and Latin America is indigenous in character. Sometimes this is a result of more recent resistance to and rejection of missionary forms from the West. Just as often, this is due to having had centuries and even millennia of developments on their own terms, quite apart from influences by the established Western/Roman Catholic and even Eastern Orthodox churches.

To be sure, during and since the arrival of missionaries accompanying the modern colonial movement, the issue has always been to what degree the presumed older and more established churches ought not to just allow but also to encourage and enable indigenous autonomy. Autonomous churches are self-supporting, self-propagating, and self-governing. These "three-self" characteristics are assumed in many respects, at least in theory, while being much more challenging in practice. On the one hand, even to take up the debate on these terms presumes a Western provenance and missionary perspective that ignores the actual self-agency of all people created in the image of God. On the other hand, even if we were to assume indigenous autonomy (which in reality is always relational and never absolute), the three-self notion includes, at least implicitly, the responsibility for self-theologizing.

If theological reflection were considered in terms of purposive inquiry motivated by curiosity or the personal search for truth, it is rather obvious that there are as many opportunities for such activity as there are individuals who embark on these paths. The freedom of conscience (that especially the Radical Reformed insisted upon) and the freedom of religion (enshrined in the constitutions of many secular and democratic states) undergird the spiritual pursuit. The traditioned character of such activity merely means that people begin from wherever they are, geographically, regionally, culturally,

> *Should the creeds of the early church be shared by all Christians, or should new Christian communities have the freedom to craft their own affirmations of faith?*

and ecclesially. One would therefore not expect that theological reflection in South or East Asia would produce the same results as when undertaken in Central or Southern Africa, or in the Caribbean, the Amazonian jungles, or the Andes, and so forth.

But rather than being merely private affairs, theological deliberations in this or that historic and geographic space sometimes come to define the beliefs and practices of the whole church, the body of Christ. In this case theological ideas become doctrinal commitments: orthodoxy. But should "local" church confessions, such as the ecumenical creeds of Nicaea-Constantinople and Chalcedon, be transmitted and translated (linguistically) across space and time, and should new ecclesial movements be impressed to embrace such as their own? In most instances Western missionaries presumed that this was part of their task. Those missionized in various contexts responded variously. Sometimes they would acquiesce with or without much fanfare. Other times they queried the matter in ways that in turn raised other dogmatic and theological questions. In a few cases new churches would outright reject the "orthodoxies" introduced by missionaries and would draft their own confessional statements. There are good arguments that the one, holy, catholic (universal), and apostolic church declared by the Nicene-Constantinopolitan Creed (see also chap. 6 below) ought to have one confession. Otherwise the claim that there is one people of God and body of Christ seems empty. Yet it is also undeniable that every creed and confession responds to specific historical and cultural circumstances and questions. If different contexts bring with them new theological opportunities, why not accept that there will also be fresh dogmatic formulations?

At the beginning of the third millennium, it is quite clear that the churches across the so-called majority world of Asia, Africa, and Latin America are at least speaking back to, if not also confronting, the more historic European and American ecclesial traditions (with Orthodox churches included on both sides of the equation). Yet there are additional complicating factors. Migration blurs East-and-West and North-and-South categories. Digitization further shrinks the distances between cultures as well as transforms human interaction, perhaps even human nature itself. Secularization has forged new post-Christendom, surely post-Christian, environments and realities that are less and less beholden to former Christian ideas and values. Within this new milieu of globalization, the church and its various traditions are changing. At the very least, the Internet is transforming the ways in which "we" argue among ourselves or with others. Similarly impacted, for millennials, spiritual excursions are now possible across cultures, even without needing to leave home physically, given the telecommunications revolution. But such cross-cultural endeavors may be precipitated also because of felt rootlessness. Such seeking leads to an openness to multiple traditions or spiritualities rather than reliance on one or a few.

If theology draws at least in part from tradition, then tradition's changing character translates into theological fluidity. Such perceived instability is aggravated rather than helped by the realization that the traditions of one's youth, if raised ecclesially at all, are one among many options, not all of them consistent. And in the contemporary global context, new alternatives continue to emerge. These are forged out of a multitude of ecclesial and historical factors, including theological and doctrinal matters.

2.4. The Spirit of Tradition in Its Contextuality

It is precisely for these reasons that committed Protestants, especially of the conservative evangelical sort, are likely to fall back onto the tradition of the *solae*, particularly *sola scriptura*. Amid the volatility of traditions ebbing and flowing in reaction to erratic historical forces, most evangelicals argue that theology needs an immovable foundation. The Bible is that secure basis upon which theological reflection stands. Such Protestants will go further. They deem as unacceptable the scriptural canons of the

> *How do Scripture and tradition fit together?*

Roman Catholic Church, which include the Apocrypha, and of other Orthodox communions that add even further deuterocanonical books. Only the sixty-six books in Protestant editions of the Bible are to be recognized as Scripture.

Two preliminary considerations are apropos. First, as indicated in the first chapter, the role of the Holy Spirit cannot be ignored in any consideration of Scripture, no matter which canon is consulted. Second, as manifest already (§2.2), *sola scriptura* leads not to a consensus but to multiplication. Even if we all read the same translation, version, or form of the Bible, that is no guarantee that we will agree theologically, much less agree doctrinally. More importantly, part of our argument here is that Scripture and tradition go together, even if the former retains authoritative priority. There is a sense in which the Bible is the ultimate arbiter of the ups and downs of tradition. Yet equally important is also the sense in which tradition, in and through all of its waxing and waning, provides the lenses through which Scripture is read, interpreted, understood, and applied. Tradition thus comes to include the receptive and effective history of the world in front of the biblical text (see §1.3). Conservative evangelicals might emphasize the first point about biblical authority. But not being alert to the second point leads to ecclesial and denominational fragmentation when disagreements arise (as both sides insist that their views are biblical, not the other's). Defenders of the role of tradition rightly point out the ways it both constrains and empowers scriptural interpretation and engagement. Still, it is never too often to be reminded that tradition can devolve and distort the gospel when not ruled according to Scripture.

What is the justification for linking tradition to the Bible in this way? In effect, the tradition of Scripture itself. Traditions of the Torah were not dismissed but amplified in the later history of ancient Israel, including when being written out of the pressures of the Babylonian exile. The Deuteronomic historian, named by scholars as the author or authors of the books of Deuteronomy through Second Kings, shows how Torah was received over time. The prophets depict how Torah was interpreted and understood. Later in Israel's history, the Wisdom literature and postexilic writings reflect how Torah is considered in relation to the traditions of other cultures. Similarly,

> *If the Spirit is always active in the church, then tradition is always growing and evolving.*

the earliest followers of Jesus as Messiah "examined the scriptures every day" (Acts 17:11) to further comprehend the message of the gospel that they heard proclaimed to them. The New Testament documents bear ample witness to how these first disciples understood their faith to be "in accordance with the scriptures" (1 Cor. 15:3–4; cf. 2 Cor. 4:13; 2 Tim. 3:16).

Scripture, then, can be understood as the unfolding of tradition, indeed as its fount. Later conciliar creeds, synodic canons, papal encyclicals, magisterial documents, ecclesial confessions, denominational statements of faith, and the like can each be received sympathetically as historical, cultural, and contextual responses to and expressions of "the faith that was once for all entrusted to the saints" (Jude 3b). All of these also can be recognized as being inevitably partial, as is all human knowledge and language. The relevance of ecumenically forged creeds to later generations more removed in time and place will fluctuate because of their contextuality even as later confessions will predictably arise to meet concrete needs under new circumstances. These articulations need not be considered in exclusivist terms. Acceptance of one may not require rejections of other/s. Even contrasting claims signal that traditions represent different perspectives, perhaps sometimes even being wrong (when both claims cannot be reconciled). But in good faith, theological efforts of church traditions aspire toward the truth, while hopefully also being open to correction.

Tradition's vitality therefore ought not to be suppressed, especially for an incarnational and pentecostal faith that believes God acts not only metaphysically but also historically, in the person of Jesus of Nazareth and through his Spirit "poured out . . . upon all flesh" (Acts 2:17). If the revelation of Scripture itself grows in clarity from the Old to the New Testaments, then there is no reason why the church and its teachings might not also continue to develop and to gain contextual illumination in ever-new times and places. In their message and practices, in fact, the various traditions, movements, and churches, even denominations, can be understood as each having distinctive gifts to contribute to the one, holy, catholic, and apostolic church. Jesus' own message pointed ahead to the fullness of the coming reign (kingdom) of God, and in this time before that arrival, our own traditioned theological musings can gain from ever-greater precision as we attend in faith to what the Spirit is saying, doing, and bringing about. This is not to baptize all development as faithful or biblical: it is obvious that some turnings of the tradition are wrongheaded and misdirected. It is to say that the church ought to expect its own reformation and renewal and to embrace its own perpetual transformation, by the power of the Spirit.

In chapter 6 we shall return to consider many of these aspects of tradition in more detail, particularly with regard to the notion of doctrinal diversity that characterizes the present global church. For the moment, it is important to note only that the preceding discussion shows how and why the theological reflections of the church's members will develop depending on historical, geographical, and cultural location. By extension, the church's teachings, those less essential and those of greater import, like its doctrines and confessions, will adjust, not in the sense of displacing former instruments but in the sense of clarifying Christian belief in changing contexts. From the perspective of faith, the members of the body of Christ must accept also that they are part of the communion and fellowship of the Holy Spirit, being led and renewed by the Spirit in love of one another and service to the world. Thus new ideas and formulations will be promoted, albeit never ones that are absolutely novel. Any innovation faithful to Scripture will retain some measure of continuity with the past even as it gestures toward a richer expression in a new moment in anticipation of the full revelation to come. Discernment of such faithfulness remains a task for the local, regional, and ecumenical, or catholic, church and involves also reasoned argumentation as well, to which we now turn.

Discussion Questions

1. How does our participation in church, whether from a young age or as relative newcomers, habituate and socialize us into a theological tradition?

2. Protestantism's protests seem to have divided us irremediably; how is it possible for the Holy Spirit to lift up God's glory out of these many (sometime opposing) tongues?

3. Does the one, holy, catholic, and apostolic church need one creed? Why or why not?

4. How does or might the Holy Spirit work in and through the traditions of the church in its many expressions?

For Further Reading

Burgess, Stanley M. *The Holy Spirit.* 3 vols. Peabody, MA: Hendrickson Publishers, 1984–94.

Congar, Yves. *The Meaning of Tradition.* New York: Hawthorne Books, 1964.

Hughes, Philip. *The Church in Crisis: A History of the General Councils, 325–1870.* Garden City, NY: Hanover House, 1961.

Irvin, Dale T. *Christian Histories, Christian Traditioning: Rendering Accounts.* Maryknoll, NY: Orbis Books, 1998.

Irvin, Dale T., and Scott W. Sunquist. *History of the World Christian Movement.* 3 vols. Maryknoll, NY: Orbis Books, 2001–19.

Leith, John H. *Creeds of the Churches: A Reader in Christian Doctrine from the Bible to the Present.* 3rd ed. Atlanta: John Knox Press, 1982.

Noll, Mark A. *Protestantism: A Very Short Introduction.* Oxford: Oxford University Press, 2011.

Pelikan, Jaroslav. *The Christian Tradition: A History of the Development of Doctrine.* 5 vols. Chicago: University of Chicago Press, 1975–90.

Russell, Jeffrey Burton, and Douglas W. Lumsden. *A History of Medieval Christianity: Prophecy and Order.* 4th ed. New York: Peter Lang, 2007.

Toon, Peter. *The Development of Doctrine in the Church.* Grand Rapids: Wm. B. Eerdmans Publishing Co., 1979.

Vanhoozer, Kevin J. *Biblical Authority after Babel: Retrieving the Solas in the Spirit of Mere Protestant Christianity.* Grand Rapids: Brazos Press, 2016.

Vondey, Wolfgang. *Pentecostalism: A Guide for the Perplexed.* New York: Bloomsbury, 2013.

Wiles, Maurice. *The Making of Christian Doctrine: A Study in the Principles of Early Doctrinal Development.* Cambridge: Cambridge University Press, 1975.

Yong, Amos, with images and commentary by Jonathan A. Anderson. *Renewing Christian Theology: Systematics for a Global Christianity.* Waco, TX: Baylor University Press, 2014.

3

Reason

Renewing the Mind in the Spirit

The preceding two chapters have shown how the Bible as theological resource is not apart from the church's traditions: cumulative traditions of the church are also sources for theology while building on the scriptural basis. In this chapter, we turn to consider the third aspect of the Anglican triad and the Wesleyan quadrilateral: reason. Similarly, as before, we will endeavor to understand reasoning as a kind of theological resource, albeit one that works with and not independently of Scripture and tradition.

This chapter traces the dominant paradigms of reasoning by beginning with the Neoplatonism of the early church period, the Aristotelian revival in the medieval church and in the scholastic movement, and the liturgical rationality of the Orthodox tradition. We then continue through the scientific revolution of the early modern era, then arrive at or into the present postmodern milieu. The final section discusses how the Holy Spirit both speaks or works through shifting and dynamic human cognitive schemes while also transcending them. For theological purposes, we can say that human rationality is pneumatologically enabled, accomplished by and through the Holy Spirit. The present chapter both argues and exemplifies this claim.

Again, as before, our consideration of reason in these next few pages precedes our discussion of experience in chapter 4. This is not because reason and experience are not entangled, but it is for the sake of clarifying first the relationship between reason and Scripture as well as tradition. Be forewarned, however, that especially the middle parts of this chapter will be the most difficult for beginning theologians, in part because of the nature of what is being discussed and in part because of the speed with which we will be moving. (Remember to consult the glossary as needed to get your bearings.) Our hope, however, is to gain perspective on the nature of human reason that we take for granted. By the time we finally arrive at the topic of experience at the end of this first part of the book, we should be well equipped to see how each aspect of the quadrilateral, while conceptually distinct, is nevertheless interrelated.

3.1. Rationality as Traditioned

If asked to think about reason, we might initially consider that human reasoning or rationality is the same everywhere and all the time. In the next section we shall see more directly why this is our default assumption. For now, having come through the discussion so far, we might not be surprised to consider reason itself as *traditioned*, as shaped by traditions of thinking. The preceding has prompted us to recognize that there are many traditions of rationality within the Christian faith. But what about beyond Christianity altogether?

For instance, our introductory chapter mentioned that Thomas Aquinas was himself attempting to sort out the recovery of the ancient fourth-century-BCE philosopher Aristotle and the legacy of his ideas. Although it is impossible to characterize in a few words the meaning of Aristotelianism as a philosophical tradition, a number of points are noteworthy. First, Thomas's own efforts were monumental precisely because Aristotle's ideas were being mediated to the Latin West by way of Islamic scholars amid the Muslim-Christian encounter of the medieval period. This alerts us to the fact that there is no single philosophical system known as Aristotelianism, but rather varying traditions of such. Thomas's endeavors were crucial for the intellectual credibility of Christian faith in a time of interreligious encounter and confrontation. Second, Thomas's own reworking and then transmission of that Greek philosopher contributed an empirical or observational aspect to the philosophical and theological methods of the medieval academy. Aristotle's attentiveness to the sense perception of things and forms was translated by Thomas into a way of learning about creaturely realities by focusing on how they appear to us, even while appreciating their ultimate relationship to God as Creator. The result is a Thomistic rationality that easily combines nature (what we experience) and grace (God's revelation), that sees a convergence between reason and faith. Thomism as a tradition of theological reason moves back and forth "from below" (the realm of creation) and "from above" (divine transcendence) in an uninhibited manner.

Not surprisingly, Aristotle's teacher, Plato, was himself a major philosopher who has inspired a number of schools of thought. Was Aristotle's more empirical temper a direct response to his teacher's more idealist sensibilities? Putting it this way is not only a potentially misleading generalization but overly dualistic. Nevertheless, the Plato-Aristotle relationship helpfully charts two trajectories of rationality that can be seen as distinct even if never unrelated. The first is a more rationalist approach that prioritizes the workings of the cosmic or divine mind and believes that ideas are more real and eternal than material things on earth, which arise and pass away. The second, in contrast, is a more empiricist perspective, emphasizing human perception and experience in space and time as generative of otherwise fleeting mental images and impressions. Biblically, there is a sense in which Platonic idealism and its suspicions about materiality and embodiment appear in parts of the New Testament, including when the apostles talk about the opposition between the spiritual and fleshly realms. At the same time, Aristotelian empiricism that focuses on what is seen and heard is consistent with the historical character of Christian beliefs in the incarnation of the Son and

> *Platonism was the tradition of reasoning that formed most of the theologians of the early church period.*

the pentecostal outpouring of the Spirit. If a Platonized Christianity is liable to the errors of Gnosticism that devalue the material creation, the problems of an Aristotelianized Christianity are exacerbated in modern cultures dominated by certain forms of scientistic empiricism, as we shall see momentarily.

Platonism, theologically, was one of the dominant philosophical handmaids to Christian tradition until Thomas. The early church fathers, including those who contributed to the ecumenical councils and creeds, were often trained in and shaped by contemporary Neoplatonist schools of thought. Christian theological debates from the second century onward deployed Greek ideas and concepts; the debaters presumed the idealistic worldview bequeathed by Plato and his philosophic descendants. God, a spiritual rather than material reality, was more easily comprehensible in terms of Plato's eternal ideas. In the New Testament, it is the *Logos*, or "Word," of ancient Greek philosophy that is associated with the divine reality and that eventually takes on human flesh (John 1:1–14).

Within the Eastern Orthodox tradition (see also §2.1), the liturgy is understood in a sacramental sense that extends this New Testament principle. The God who takes on flesh to reveal ultimate truth to finite creatures also condescends to the liturgical practices of the church to save and sanctify the people of God. Yet the liturgy enacted in the Spirit being poured out on all flesh can also become, here understood in Neoplatonic fashion, an icon or window into the eternal and unchanging divine reality. Thus we see that Orthodox spirituality habituates human hearts, orienting them through the repetitive acts of worship to the unseen Deity and eternal truths. The Orthodox tradition Platonically infused therefore appreciates creaturely activity, especially when liturgically enacted in embodied worship albeit always as ordered toward the spiritual and transcendent domain.

So far, we have attempted to depict how Christian theological traditions have distinct rationalities, whether shaped by the idealism of Platonist philosophy or by the empiricism of Aristotelian traditions. That the latter's reliance on experience is a type of reasoning will be more apparent in the next section. Yet for the moment this means neither that Roman Catholicism is merely Aristotelian nor that Orthodoxy is simply Platonist in rational orientation. This is impossible because such philosophical traditions are multiple in themselves. And Christian traditions like the Latin West and the Orthodox East also are diversely constituted. On this point, to the degree that Catholicism and Orthodoxy are "global" traditions, as already indicated (see §2.3 above), they are shaped by non-Western philosophies as well. South Asian Christians of all stripes, including Protestants, are influenced by Hindu and Buddhist philosophical traditions with all of their contestations. Comparatively, East Asian churches have to do additionally with evolving Confucian and Daoist ways of life and thinking.

It is too simplistic, then, to contrast Western and Eastern rationalities as opposite. There is a grain of truth to saying that the former is structured by either-or choices and the latter is modulated variously by yin-yang or both-and harmonies. But in the end, such traditions are too complex and resist such contrasting categorization. Platonism or Aristotelianism as philosophies and Christianity as a religious tradition are multifarious phenomena. Therefore we need to be aware of how Christians in very different places and cultures think and reason in their own unique "Western," "Eastern," or hybrid ways. This does not mean that Christians cannot understand one another. It means only that we cannot assume they always mean the same thing even when using the same words, particularly when we working with linguistic translations. In short, human reason is historically formed, shaped by various cultural, linguistic, and religious factors.

3.2. Scientific Revolution, the Enlightenment, and Universal Reason

The empirical mentality flowered in multiple directions after the scholastic period, including during the Renaissance movement, in the wake of which also appeared some of the early figures of modern science like Nicolaus Copernicus (1473–1543) and Galileo Galilei (1564–1642). The so-called Copernican revolution formally proposed that the ancient Ptolemaic system's envisioning the earth as the center of the universe, around which the heavens moved, did not fit the facts. Meanwhile the competing heliocentric theory that the earth and other planets revolved around the sun was extensively debated, leading to the condemnation and imprisonment of Galileo, one of its chief proponents. That heliocentrism finally prevailed reflects at least in part the gradual if inexorable advance of the scientific method, based upon experiential observation, inductive experimentation, and empirical testing and (dis)confirmation.

One facet of the modern scientific mind sought human enlightenment. Enlightened reason worked to replace premodern myths, beliefs, and "superstitions," even those of religious provenance, with demonstrable knowledge and proven "facts." Galileo's trial, led by the religious authorities of his day, fueled the putative "warfare" between science and religion. Those who promulgate such a battle ignore the fact that

> *Scientific and religious knowledge can be seen as complementary rather than in competition with one another.*

only small groups in both camps were responsible for the opposition. Far on the one side are scientific positivists who believe truth is accessible only through empirical experimentation. Equally distant on the other side are religious conservatives who are convinced that the former is godless and ignores the limitations of the scientific method. In between lies the majority of those who in some respect hold science and religion together, whether by dealing with them as disparate (material and spiritual) domains of reality or by assuming that scientific and religious knowledge are complementary.

Alongside this tradition of modern science has been the parallel development of modern philosophy. Early modern thinkers like René Descartes (1596–1650) suggested that human reason ought to be critically examined and all ideas should be secured on rational foundations, rather than received on prior authority. What is indubitable is that *thought* exists and therefore also that *thinkers* exist. Thus Descartes's famous *Cogito ergo sum*, "I think, therefore I am," was accepted as providing a new, indisputable foundation for knowledge. Such Cartesian skepticism, driven by methodological doubt, would clear away many preconceived assumptions and reestablish human knowing on a more secure footing. Yet at the heart of the Cartesian enterprise was a troubling gap: the gulf between the subject of thinking and the object of thought. Descartes himself posited that the link was to be found in the pineal gland, the objective location where the subjective consciousness of doubting-thinking human souls resided.

Cartesian (skeptical) rationalism was not inconsistent with the emerging philosophical empiricism. English philosopher John Locke (1632–1704) urged that the human mind was a *tabula rasa*, or blank slate, rather than endowed with innate ideas, such as in Descartes's *cogito*. Locke therefore proposed an empirical analysis of experience that he understood as complementing Cartesian rationalism in seeking to purify the mind from unfounded abstractions. Locke's approach found its radical extreme in David Hume (1711–76), who urged that our thinking capacities nevertheless cannot bridge the gulf between our experience and the external world. Hume also asserted that the connection between the two is based on how we are habituated or socialized therein. Reason is therefore not just experiential but also affective, passional, and emotional. Reason is driven by our habits and their successes in crisscrossing the world. Hume's position was, arguably, the logical end result of Cartesian doubt and Lockean empiricism combined.

These streams converged in the German philosopher Immanuel Kant (1724–1804), who sought a way beyond Hume's skepticism. Kant urged that what we know is structured not by innate ideas (as bequeathed by the Platonic tradition) but by the mind's categorical capacities, for instance, the spatial and temporal character and cause-and-effect nature of human experience. As such, human perception and thought are mediated by our interaction with the *phenomenal* world—in other words, the world that appears to our senses. In that sense, the Cartesian subject-object dualism is redefined. On the one side are our mental concepts forged in experience. On the other side are the essences or realities of things but as they exist in themselves, inaccessible to our minds. The result is a kind of Kantian agnosticism about that which transcends human conceptualization, here granting Hume his due. On the other hand, Kant's empiricist sensibilities and rationalist commitments combined to make possible a synthetic via media. Rather than acquiescing to Humean passional reason, for Kant human rationality is ultimately about navigating a world with other creatures like ourselves, thereby giving reason a practical and moral dimension. The latter involves Kant's *categorical imperative*: that human creatures act in ways and according to principles that can and should be applied to all others, including themselves. Thus we ought not to hurt other people since we would not want others to hurt us. This moral aspect of practical reason leads to Kant's religious philosophy. Theism (belief in God or the gods) thereby emerges as a postulate of practical rationality, undergirding the categorical imperative not as any requirement of reason but as a preexisting assumption.

Across the English Channel from the continent, some leading Scottish philosophers were also forging a response to the Cartesian and Humean doubt, in small part also as an alternative to the agnosticism persisting in Kant's critical philosophy. Known also as Scottish Common Sense Realism, the central notion is that knowledge is as given to us in our basic experiences of the world. Rather than incapacitating or enervating, human knowing is empowering. There is every reason to be confident, given the successes of scientific discovery and the advances of human civilizations, that our experiential and commonsensical interpretation of the world is fundamentally trustworthy.

We have covered much ground in intellectual history in a very short space. The emergence of the modern mind, as the preceding barely indicates, features epistemological (the study of knowing) twists and turns, not to say convoluted debates. Arguably, however, no matter how the philosophical disputes continue, the modern university exemplifies the epitome of human reason. In this context the "normal" features of rationality are that it is manifest in and guided by the scientific method, and these are believed to be common to all human experience (hence their presumed universality). The modern university's replication within and also outside the Western world is indicative of the extent to which its values, that concerning its historical understandings of reason and rationality also, have impressed themselves across the transcultural human landscape.

3.3. Postmodern (Ir)Rationalities(!)

The perpetual advance for humankind believed to be possible through modern science came crashing down, however, over the course of two world wars during the first part of the twentieth century. The turn-of-the-twentieth-century thinkers came to believe that the so-called power of human reason was anything but objective. Instead, reason was driven by the underlying unconscious, or the will to political power, or by revolutionary violence in the socioeconomic realm (wherein the have-nots would rise up against the haves in a potentially never-ending cycle). Out of the rubble of the Second World War also came the cry for emancipation of the colonized nations. Later dubbed the postcolonial revolution, this upheaval signaled the revolt against Western and colonial ways of life and thinking intended to displace indigenous cultural practices and traditions. Since then, the emergence of these non-Western voices and perspectives on the world stage has been facilitated by the forces of globalization and migration and by the development of electronic telecommunication. It is not that modern science was rejected or that the modern university was overthrown. Rather, Western models for such undertakings are understood as historical and contextual, and not as exclusive of non-Western efforts. Hence the legacy of the scientific Enlightenment was now contested by the revival and resurgence of many indigenous cultures across Asia, Africa, and Latin America.

Amid the postcolonial upheaval in the mid-1960s, civil rights movements starting in the West and then spreading elsewhere quickly demanded justice

for persons marginalized in their societies due to race, ethnicity, socioeconomic class standing, and also disability (see also §4.2). Interwoven across the
board amid these developments were the sexual revolution and the emergence of feminism as a sociopolitical force. This was not just about voting
rights, already secured in many Western nations, but also about political
voice and economic equality in a heretofore male-dominated or patriarchally
ordered world. For our purposes, feminist perspectives argued that the so-
called universality of modern reason emphasized the mind's conceptual and
analytic capacities but did not account for
the role of embodiment in human thinking. This feminist notion, popularized
in terms of "left brain" (male) logic and
"right brain" (female) intuition, exagger-
ated the differences between men and
women. More recent neuroscientific and related studies have shown that the
brain's division of labor is not as clear-cut as in this demarcation. But there is
no denying the emotional and affective dimension to human rationality that
roots our cognition in brain and bodily processes. Yes, there are subtle varia-
tions in male and female ways of knowing modulated by embodied patterns,
social relations, and cultural factors. Postcolonial and the postpatriarchal systems of thought were therefore interrelated.

> *Abstract, universal reason has been replaced by particular, local narratives.*

Alongside postcolonialism and postpatriarchalism was also postmodernism. Given the effective fragmentation of Enlightenment reason, the so-
called modern mind was increasingly understood in the widely heralded
postmodern milieu as postinstrumental (not reducible to scientific advance)
but more recently also as posttechnological (mediated but not dominated by
electronic digitization). If modernity was equated, in one account, to scientific and universal reason, then postmodernity's insurgency, in a contrasting
narrative, was the dissolution of the so-called metanarrative into its many
local stories. Modern objectivity, hence, disintegrates into postmodern subjectivity, denoting the resounding of the many voices that fractures the scientific rationality of the West. The modern mind, then, signified by the (white)
European male has given way to the postmodern individual-in-community,
the non(white)-European person and group, including females. The abstract
and universal metarationality is also being displaced by competing local narratives. The latter are historically situated, culturally contextual, and socially
(not to mention biologically) embodied. Reason is thus valued not only in
argumentative (written) treatises undergirded by Western literacy but also in
other forms or genres of human communication such as poetry, fiction, and
the full spectrum of the creative arts.

These postcolonial, postpatriarchal, and postmodern ways of seeing the world are also post-Christian. They are certainly post-Christendom insofar as the latter denoted the fusion of religion and the state that marked the colonial expansion beyond the European West. Yet the American experiment of disentangling church and state marked the major opening toward the separation of the religious and political domains of late modern (and postmodern) society. Within Western cultures, then, indigenous or native traditions long subordinated were revitalized. The demise of Christendom as a political contract between the church and the state thus also opened up to the possibility of post-Christian social systems. In the mid-twentieth century, many expected this development to result in thoroughly secular societies. But now, instead of a nonreligious and secular public square, we instead are seeing the emergence of a religiously filled *polis*, or public space. Accelerated by the forces of globalization, not only indigenous or native spiritualities but also the major world religions have spread and surged,

> *We now see that reason is formed historically, socially, culturally, and politically by its context.*

frequently bumping into one another and in the process complicating public life. Islam as a world religion is expanding beyond the regions where it has remained for over a millennium and into Western societies. At the same time, Asian adherents and devotees are bringing Confucian, Buddhist, and Hindu traditions along their diasporic routes. As colonial efforts transported Christian faith to the majority world, so postcolonial migration is bringing other religions to the Western hemisphere.

The point is that the form of scientific and Enlightenment rationality extended by Western colonizers in the last few hundred years is now contested by the individualisms of late modern Western societies and by the range of indigenous-cultural forms of life and their ways of thinking. Scientific inquiry continues, although chastened by attention to cultural variables and increasingly cognizant of its limitations (that empirical methods can observe the material world but not what may lie beyond it). Rationality and reason are not just one thing; they arise within separate communities and form distinct traditions, which then compete with and complement one another. Authoritative pronouncements, even by the scientific academy, are now contested and contestable. When in some contexts these many voices inhibit communication, some perceive the postmodern condition as *irrational* rather than as a form of reasonableness. Given the plurality of discourses (rationalities) operative now in the contemporary public square, some fear a paralyzing relativism that disallows moral, religious, and other commitments.

But instead of a situation of relativism, what we have is a *contextualism* that considers reasoned argumentation to be formed historically, socially, culturally, and politically by its context. For us, of course, this is an essential theological question: if even rationality is contextual, can we arrive at truth?

3.4. The Reasoning Spirit

To put the question quite that way is itself a legacy of the modern mind: either truth or relativism. Yet as our passage so far has sought to reveal, modernity's neat disjunctions are no longer as compelling in our late modern or postmodern context. Even more pertinent, relativism is less of a concern for late modern and postmodern persons awakened to historical consciousness and aware of the role that context plays in our understanding of reason. If the middle sections of this chapter have been somewhat dense, part of the reason may be that they too quickly overview philosophical developments more ensconced in academia than directly connected to the church and its mission in and to the world. And this itself is also a bifurcation foisted by this version of the Western philosophical tradition, thus highlighting its own contextual character, at least for late modern or postmoderns with eyes to see or ears to hear otherwise.

Yet our objective is not to dismiss rationality but to situate it historically in order that we can salvage it for theological purposes. From a biblical perspective, one might argue that there is a scriptural rationality, one framed by the drama of creation-fall-and-redemption while being constituted by the biblical witness. Thus scriptural reason functions not according to the universalized metanarrative of modern Enlightenment science but according to its own resources. But scriptural logic, I want to be clear, is not somehow parochial or exclusivistic in any narrow sense. For instance, the wisdom traditions of ancient Israel—Job, Proverbs, and Ecclesiastes at the heart of the Hebrew canon—include adaptations of other cultural sayings, insights, and perspectives. These show that the people of Yahweh were not averse to borrowing from their neighbors. Daniel and his compatriots were "versed in every branch of wisdom, endowed with knowledge and insight, and competent to serve in the king's palace; they were to be taught the literature and language of the Chaldeans" (Dan. 1:4b). Before him, as Stephen the martyr was recorded as saying, "Moses was instructed in all the wisdom of the Egyptians and was powerful in his words and deeds" (Acts 7:22).

To be sure, the Pauline tradition in particular also cautions hearers, "Do not be conformed to this world, but be transformed by the renewing of your minds" (Rom. 12:2a). Paul also urges believers to "destroy arguments and every proud obstacle raised up against the knowledge of God, and . . . take every thought captive to obey Christ" (2 Cor. 10:4b–5). Last but not least, he warns, "See to it that no one takes you captive through philosophy and empty deceit, according to human tradition, according to the elemental spirits of the universe, and not according to Christ" (Col. 2:8). For Paul, there was a substantive difference between "plausible words of wisdom" and the "demonstration of the Spirit and of power," in other words between "human wisdom" and "the power of God" (1 Cor. 2:4–5). The former is worldly, based on accepted intellectual ingenuity, socially valued standing, and conventionally lauded achievements (see 1 Cor. 1:19–31), but these are "doomed to perish" (1 Cor. 2:6b). God's wisdom, however, precedes that of this age and is revealed to the people of God by the divine Spirit (1 Cor. 2:7–8, 10–13).

Paul summarizes his line of thinking this way: "Those who are unspiritual do not receive the gifts of God's Spirit, for they are foolishness to them, and they are unable to understand them because they are spiritually discerned. Those who are spiritual discern all things, and they are

> *Our common humanity, enabled by the Spirit, underlies our capacity to think, reason, and know.*

themselves subject to no one else's scrutiny. 'For who has known the mind of the Lord so as to instruct him?' But we have the mind of Christ" (1 Cor. 2:14–16, citing Isa. 40:13, Greek Septuagint).

This Pauline position emphasizes the distinctiveness of divinely granted wisdom that contrasts with human rational capacity on its own. It is consistent with the prophetic admonition:

> For my thoughts are not your thoughts,
>   nor are your ways my ways, says the LORD.
> For as the heavens are higher than the earth,
>   so are my ways higher than your ways
>   and my thoughts than your thoughts.
>   (Isa. 55:8–9)

Yet Paul himself realizes that human creatures know in part because they are spiritually constituted. This is clear in his rhetorical question: "What human being knows what is truly human except the human spirit that is within?" (1 Cor. 2:11a). This assumption relies on the Hebrew Bible testimony to the fact that the same wind of God that hovered over the primordial creation was also breathed into the dust that became Adamic humanity (Gen. 1:2; 2:7), and that the removal of this divine wind leads to creaturely demise (see Job 33:4; 34:14–15; Ps. 104:29–30). In other words, there is a common humanity enabled by the breath of God that underlies our capacity to think, reason, and know.

Noteworthy then is that the Spirit's outpouring on all flesh at Pentecost enables cross-cultural communication amid the confusion. The many languages across creaturely space and time enable, in this context, "speaking about God's deeds of power" (Acts 2:11b). The Pentecost event manifests a multiconversational rationality bearing witness to the coming reign (kingdom) of God. In the postmodern climate, linguistic plurality differentiates cultural forms of rationality. If for some people such diversity and pluralism are part of a fallen world that needs to be overcome, our understanding is that the miracle of Pentecost reveals the possibility that the many types of human reasoning evidenced across cultural-linguistic systems are being and will be finally (eschatologically) redeemed. In other words, in contrast to the homogeneity of modern reason, Pentecost announces the full flourishing of human cultures according to their many tongues and languages. It is not that objectivity and subjectivity are blurred but that they are reconstituted by the intersubjectivity of many voices enabled by the divine breath. In this case, biblically recognized wisdom is constituted by, rather than dismissive of, many ecclesial traditions and cultural societies, albeit as transfigured in Christ through his Holy Spirit.

Discussion Questions

1. How would you characterize the differences between, let's say, Protestant and Roman Catholic rationality?
2. What are the strengths of modern scientific reason or of the rationality of the modern university? What are their attendant weaknesses?
3. What are the contributions, if any, of postcolonial, postpatriarchal, and postmodern perspectives? How are these positions themselves contextually limited in relationship to the colonial, patriarchal, and modern realities they are supposedly *after*?
4. Do you think that the Spirit who speaks in and through many tongues at Pentecost provides a way for conversation and argument in a pluralistic world?

For Further Reading

Bass, Dorothy C., et al. *Christian Practical Wisdom: What It Is, Why It Matters*. Grand Rapids: Wm. B. Eerdmans Publishing Co., 2016.
Coakley, Sarah, ed. *Faith, Rationality, and the Passions.* Malden, MA: Wiley-Blackwell, 2012.
Coulter, Dale M., and Amos Yong, eds. *The Spirit, the Affections, and the Christian Tradition*. Notre Dame, IN: University of Notre Dame Press, 2016.
Kreeft, Peter. *Philosophy 101 by Socrates: An Introduction to Philosophy via Plato's "Apology."* South Bend, IN: St. Augustine's Press, 2012.

Kwok, Pui-Lan. *Postcolonial Imagination and Feminist Theology*. Louisville, KY: Westminster John Knox Press, 2005.

Livingston, James C. *Modern Christian Thought from the Enlightenment to Vatican II*. New York: Macmillan, 1971.

MacIntyre, Alasdair. *Whose Justice? Which Rationality?* Notre Dame, IN: University of Notre Dame Press, 1988.

Peterson, John. *An Introduction to Thomistic Philosophy*. Lanham, MD: University Press of America, 2012.

Smith, James K. A. *Thinking in Tongues: Pentecostal Contributions to Christian Philosophy*. Grand Rapids: Wm. B. Eerdmans Publishing Co., 2010.

Van Huyssteen, J. Wentzel. *The Shaping of Rationality: Toward Interdisciplinarity in Theology and Science*. Grand Rapids: Wm. B. Eerdmans Publishing Co., 1999.

Westphal, Merold. *Whose Community? Which Interpretation? Philosophical Hermeneutics for the Church*. Grand Rapids: Baker Academic, 2009.

Yong, Amos. *The Dialogical Spirit: Christian Reason and Theological Method for the Third Millennium*. Eugene, OR: Cascade Books, 2014.

4

Experience

Life in, by, and through the Spirit

Those who have stayed with the discussion so far ought not to be surprised that turning attention to the notion of *experience* now means at least that we will consider this aspect of the human condition in relationship also to Scripture, tradition, and reason. From a Christian perspective, all experience is variously informed, not least by these other elements of the quadrilateral. But isn't there just a common human experience regardless of one's religious background? Just as we said that reason is both local and universal, in what follows we will see that, when it comes to theology, the answer to the question of a common human experience is *yes* and also *no*.

Our discussion here begins with human aesthetic and moral socialization and then examines life from an intersectional (involving gender/sexuality, race/ethnicity, etc.) perspective. The third section considers how encounter of and then conversion by the Spirit provides experiential grounding for theological reflection. Clearly our scope will touch on and draw upon areas already introduced previously. This is in part unavoidable since, as already indicated, the divisions of the quadrilateral are interrelated and enable consideration of theology's sources from four directions. The final section will attempt to bring together, in pneumatological perspective, the threads of the quadrilateral presented in the four chapters of part I of this book.

If we are successful, we shall have gotten a decent grasp of how the sources of theology—Scripture, tradition, reason, and experience—shape us and how we in some sense participate in them, even if mostly unconsciously. The second part of this book will invite us to think more intentionally about how we can therefore channel what is available to us for constructive purposes, including for theological reflection as young and aspiring theologians. Naming and understanding these sources turns them into resources amenable to the important task of faithful and Spirit-filled discipleship in God's world.

4.1. Socialization

What is *experience*? Clearly, infants have experiences, of cuddling at Mother's breast or laughing with Father and making noises with siblings. These are not, however, directly accessible personal resources for theology even if we might reflect on them at second hand (by observing such phenomena as young theologian, for instance). Experience that is relevant for any theological endeavor is that which finds its way into conscious articulation, however inchoate. For that matter, experience that is recognized as having personal relevance is that which comes to and is retained in consciousness, whether lodged in memory or expressed in speech (or writing). Such significant experience, therefore, has linguistic quality, and at least in that respect it can also be understood as being traditioned.

Human socialization, therefore, provides the parameters for understanding our experience and surely for expressing such to ourselves and to others. From our parents or guardians, we learn language, and such language provides a means of self-communication and self-representation. From our environment of primary and extended family, friends of the family, and others we learn about what is good ("yes!") and bad ("no!"), what is beautiful ("nice!") or ugly ("ugh!"), what to pursue (for which we are rewarded) and avoid (for which we are reprimanded and punished), what benefits us (brings us pleasure) or harms us (brings us unease or displeasure). In general, it might be that Kant's categorical imperative—that human beings act in ways and according to principles that can and should be applied to all others, including themselves (see §3.2 above)—underlies the ethical worldview that we grow up in. But more probably, such a guideline, if consciously understood at all, is mediated through the sociocultural mores that are popularly formulated and handed down from generation to generation.

As we grow older, most of us go to day care (even if with extended family), next to kindergarten, then to elementary school. In these contexts we are opened up to influences beyond the family. This is in part why some parents homeschool their children, because they are concerned that their values and perspectives might not be shared in these wider environments. For similar reasons, homeschooled children may not have access to other cultural productions such as what is available on public or cable television, or on the Internet. Further, many parents or guardians allow their children to develop friendships only with others drawn from a communal circle of families whom the parents trust to have moral (and other) convictions similar to the parents' own. The point is that socialization shapes experience and identity. What we watch on TV, who we hang out with, the teachers or other authority figures we interact with—all impact our lives. These experiences inform what we think and feel and also shape how we respond.

Along the way, we might be a bit rebellious. More intense expressions of such might lead to dropping out of high school, for example, for many reasons. But such is more common when social expectations garnered from the broader world come into conflict with family norms and values. Here experience becomes confusing, and we struggle to find a way forward, sometimes unsuccessfully. Yet such processes, no matter how they turn out, become experientially internalized. If the struggle is intense or we experience tragedy, we look for ways to avoid similar futures. The smoother our paths in life, the more "normal" we believe our experience is, and this in turn shapes our expectations of and relating to others.

There are multiple levels, as ought to be clear, of experiential formation: our family, the extended community (of kinship group and friends), and wider cultural institutions (educational, literary, communicative, etc.). As already intimated, sometimes—oftentimes!—experience is the discovery that others have different and even contrary expectations. In that regard, we are constantly negotiating a growing awareness that what we had taken for granted at a

> *Experience is the socialization that frames our way of understanding the world.*

prior stage is not at all presumed in different times, places, or contexts. Now when we factor religion into the matrix, none of this disappears; rather, these tensions just get stronger.

There is a certain sense in which religious socialization, if it happens at all at an early age, will be within environments with which parents are largely in agreement. However, even that is not always the case, particularly in our contemporary postdenominational time when families join congregational communities less because of ecclesial affiliation and name and more because of other circumstantial factors. In these cases, more often than not, families might find their prior religious, spiritual, and theological assumptions marginalized or even challenged, perhaps to the point of having to relocate their families to another church. In any event, our experiences in churches, growing up or as adults, shape our theological imagination. What is standard or less essential, what is acceptable or questionable, or what is possible or to be excluded—all these are experientially derived. We gain facility with these theological notions variously, depending on what kinds of churches we attend, who the pastors or leaders are, what is proclaimed from the pulpit or transmitted in congregational materials and resources and Web sites, and how well we listen during services or observe the lives of fellow believers, and so forth. If our church leaders espouse very strict forms of Christian practice and adhere to more conservative interpretations of the tradition's historic beliefs, we will either embrace them (and become conservative also) or replace them (if our experiences lead us to believe that such views are not helpful for life experiences outside that community). On the other hand, if we are primed by a more liberal and progressive message, we might follow suit (become liberals ourselves, but perhaps in some circumstances wishing we had deeper commitments). Or we might decide that such expressions of the faith are insufficient for some of life's situations and find more conservative churches for fellowship, groups that support more definitive rather than ambivalent stances to the world. Or any number of other unpredictable paths might evolve depending on the choices we exercise amid the experiences we encounter and the constraints we face.

Experience, in short, is the socialization (formation for life in society), even ecclesialization (formation for life in the church, if we were nurtured in and stayed within churches), that shapes our frames of reference. Life experience is the ongoing process of deconstructing and reconstructing, to the degree possible, these cognitive schemes as we encounter new or even opposing realities and perspectives. Sometimes our capacities to adjust reach a limit, and we draw boundaries over which crossing is prohibited, at least for a time. Most often, we bracket what we cannot render consistent with existing convictions and hope we are not forced to make a decision before we feel ready to commit ourselves.

4.2. Intersectionality

I now wish to burrow into topics already broached above in our discussion of postmodern rationalities (§3.3): the role of gender, race, and disability. In this present context, however, our approach is from the experiential dimension. We will draw from theories of intersectionality to show that each of these domains interacts and interfaces with the others so that experience is doubly or triply complicated.

Modern society, not to mention modern rationality, prioritizes and centralizes white, male, heterosexual, and able-bodied experience. (Those in the disability community talk about the *temporarily able-bodied*, on which more in a moment.) So the experience of women is secondary, considered if inserted into the broader conversation, but otherwise often overlooked if not ignored. Surely the experiences of males differ from that of females, so that is not the issue. What is at stake are social conventions and expectations, and their accompanying ethical implications. Whether women should receive equal pay for equal work might not be debated directly today (although such equality certainly remains unachieved). But whether or not women can do the same work as men, or have access to the same jobs or positions, continues to be contentious, not least in Christian settings.

The question is this: should female experience be explicitly factored into theology? The counterissue is that the main lines of the theological tradition have been developed by males, not only

> *Christians are called to a fully egalitarian and just order in Christ, recognizing and valuing both male and female differences, as well as linguistic, cultural, and racial-ethnic identities.*

in ways oblivious to female realities but, more importantly, having oppressive consequences for the lives of girls and women. Some might grant that in these respects, we need women's perspectives just during this interim period of working to enact more just relations between all persons. The ongoing concern, however, is that experience itself is gendered, however conscious (for women) or unconscious (for most men) we might be of it. Therefore, ongoing dialogue, consultation, and collaboration between men and women are essential to the theological task.

But what if one is a nonwhite female? In that case, one's experiences are doubly removed from the mainstream, even as nonwhite males also find themselves on the margins of their respective conversations. The issue is that, because of the colonial enterprise, European values have been exported to and impressed upon the rest of the world, in the process subordinating other cultural perspectives. Whiteness has become privileged and normative, with blackness—signifying Africa and its diasporic realities, including that transferred via the Middle Passage of the slave trade to the "new world"—at the bottom of the social hierarchy. In between are the shades of "yellowness" and "brownness," representing Asian and Latin American experiences more generally. The author of the Letter to the Colossians did write, "There is no longer Greek and Jew, circumcised and uncircumcised, barbarian, Scythian, slave and free; but Christ is all and in all!" (Col. 3:11). Thus some argue that race and ethnicity (being Greek or Jew) no longer matter. But so arguing overlooks both the fact that the colonial legacy was based and built on the experience of whites (white privilege) and that the centers of economic and cultural production continue to reside primarily in the Euro-American West (white control). Hence the Pauline dictum "There is no longer Jew or Greek, there is no longer slave or free, there is no longer male and female; for all of you are one in Christ Jesus" (Gal. 3:28) ought to be understood neither as eliminating the need to consider the gendered character of experience nor as advocating some kind of nonracial and nonethnic "colorblind" stance. Rather, Christians who hold these texts as authoritative are instead called to a fully egalitarian and just order in Christ, an order that recognizes and values both male and female differences and the particularities of their linguistic, cultural, and racial-ethnic identities. The point here is not to condemn white males but to recognize how the historical developments of Euro-American culture and transnational patriarchalism have inhibited, even if in some instances unintentionally, the prospering of others. Only recognition of this history makes possible a path of reparation and redemption for all.

This is easier said than done, however, since experience is so particular, and all the more so when one is not just nonwhite and female but also impaired or disabled in some respect. In disability studies literature, *impairments* are usually considered in relationship to the biological or sensory aspects of human bodies and capacities. *Disabilities*, by extension, are reckoned in terms of their social consequences (e.g., visual impairment means that one is handicapped in obtaining employment as a sports referee). Impairments that are invisible allow such individuals to "pass," at least until their affected capacities are exposed as subpar in social interactions. Yet to be nonwhite, female, and impaired is to be triply marginalized, just as to be white, female, and disabled is to be doubly jeopardized, or to be white, male, and disabled is still to be deviant from the established social conventions. Some might argue further that to be intellectually disabled, whether because of congenital impairments like trisomy 21 (Down syndrome) or because of later-onset impairments like mental illness, exacerbates the vulnerability of disabled experience. There is also a fine line between such later-onset mental impairments and those of later life, not just Alzheimer's and related conditions but also their associated physical impairments. But often these are not defined as disability-related and are considered as part of the aging process. Whether due to aging, biological predisposition, or contingencies of life (accidents, wars, or other impairment-conducive events), and even if not physically or sensorially impaired, human creatures come into the world dependent on others and inevitably become more and more dependent again at some point during their lives, thus the temporality of being able-bodied. Unavoidable in disability conversations and considerations are the additional layers of stigma, ostracism, and peril related to those with biological deviations related to sexuality. Homosexual, transgendered, and intersexed persons are the most prominent. Here we are discussing the intersectional characteristic of experience, not yet their political or theological aspects. The point is that whatever we decide in these latter domains ought to be supported by careful consideration of the lived realities or experienced perspectives of such persons.

Experience, in short, is multitiered; who we are is shaped by our families, our churches, and our societies. Yet in the current world order, experiences are also hierarchically evaluated according to the predominant white, male, temporarily able-bodied, heterosexual standards. The experiences of all other persons are measured according to these cultural and political conventions, acknowledged or not. Yet even with all of this layeredness, there is one additional factor when reviewed in Christian theological perspective: what pertains to the brokenness and distortions introduced by sin into the orders of creation.

4.3. Encountering the Living God, Experiencing Redemption

The Christian doctrine of sin calls attention to the fallenness of the world and its creatures, and more specifically to human rebellion against God's intentions. As much as this theological proposition must be further unpacked, grasping its truth involves experiencing its reality within the depths of the human condition. Our wills are then perceived as being misdirected according to our selfish ambitions. Our minds further realize their impairment because of and by our insurrectionist aspirations. Last but not least, our hearts feel deformed and misshapen due to distorted inclinations. As such, human life at the personal, communal, and social levels will be experienced as tragically misaligned with the divine purposes. In effect, the patriarchalism, racism/ethnocentrism, ableism, and sexism of our world can be recognized as symptoms of a human sociality profoundly tarnished and marred by sin.

> *To have Christian experience is to have met and been transformed by Jesus Christ through his Holy Spirit in some fundamental way.*

Theology as an intellectual task may, arguably, be undertaken by anyone, Christian or not, interested in the consideration of theism and things divine. Jews, Muslims, and Hindus surely engage in explicitly theological reflection even as those of other faiths border on theological endeavors. Even agnostics and atheists are on theological voyages when they argue that God does not exist (technically, what they are doing is *a*-theology). But Christian theologizing presumes some kind of Christian experience and its concomitant theological and doctrinal explications. As such, no discussion of the role of experience in theology can or should avoid considering the specifically Christian elements or aspects of religious experience.

After all, to have had some kind of religious experience, however generic, is to have developed the cultural and linguistic capacities to talk about our encounter with the transcendent realm. To have Christian experience, more particularly, is to have met and been transformed by Jesus Christ through his Holy Spirit in some fundamental way. The ashamed begin to experience acceptance and esteem in Christ. The guilty receive forgiveness. The shattered encounter healing, miraculous or gradual. The oppressed are delivered and set on the road to liberation. The poor glimpse hope. The downtrodden are uplifted in love. Those alone and estranged are reconciled to themselves, others, and their Creator. In short, lives racked and wrecked by sin are turned around by redemption in Christ through the Spirit.

Christian experience, however, is shaped by specific church traditions, each with implications for theological orientation and temperament. Participants in Orthodox, Roman Catholic, Anglican, or more formal liturgies are initiated into the communion of saints. The iconography that structures the experience of the liturgy helps us to experience a transgenerational form of congregational worship. A kind of sacramental imagination is instilled as more or less ritualized bodily responses in catechism, baptism, and weekly (or more often) eucharistic celebrations, which attune the soul to saving grace. Chants and prayers resound, incense pervades, and human hearts are caught up sacramentally and liturgically in the drama of salvation, in union with the triune God (however dimly perceived), in fellowship with their predecessors, and in anticipation of realizing the promise of and to their children (the next generation). The theologian is formed and transformed herein via periodic (usually weekly, but sometimes more or less often) liturgical repetition, affectively reoriented in the recesses of the heart to the vision of the triune God. Our lives are touched, and sinfulness is healed in worship.

Those in classical Reformation churches and tradition are also sacramentally shaped yet first and foremost through the preaching of the Word of God. In some of these churches Eucharist, or the Lord's Supper, plays a central (even if secondary) role. In contemporary evangelical circles, the Supper is more intermittent. Nevertheless, for Protestants, the order of weekly worship leads up to and revolves around the proclamation of Scripture. The Bible is read (although this public reading of the sacred text is increasingly minimal even in Protestant services) and expounded upon. Then the congregation is given opportunity to respond, either symbolically after the sermon but also in the invitation to live out their lives (that week) by obeying the divine Word. In addition, Protestant spirituality is surrounded by Scripture through regular devotional reading of the Bible, scriptural memorization, and ongoing personal meditation on the Word of God. The theologian is formed therein via (daily, in the ideal path of Protestant discipleship) literary engagement, cognitively informed and transformed in our minds in accordance with Christ as revealed in the Bible. Our minds are renewed so that sinful patterns of thinking are corrected by the Word of Christ in the power of the Holy Spirit.

At the beginning of the third millennium, the fastest-growing forms of Christianity around the world are those of the pentecostal and charismatic type. As these are found across the Orthodox, Catholic, and Protestant spectrum, they are strangers to neither the formal liturgy nor the sacrament of the Word. Yet pentecostal and charismatic spirituality is characterized by an intensified sense of openness to the signs and wonders of the Spirit. These can be miraculous experiences of healing, or they can be the subtler but no less pronounced hearing of the divine breath's whispers, even through "a sound of sheer silence" (1 Kgs. 19:12b)! But in any case these are representative of the surprising work of the Spirit, always bringing about the unexpected and unpredictable salvation of God to begin again. Pentecostal-charismatic spirituality thus expects and waits for the ongoing manifestation of the Holy Spirit through the charismata. These spiritual gifts are first and foremost for the edification of members of the body of Christ (1 Cor. 12). They enable personal testimony and empower Christian witness to others, even "to the ends of the earth" (Acts 1:8). Since the Spirit can show up at any time, the theologian is formed therein through moment-by-moment participation in the ministry and mission of the Spirit of Pentecost. The human spirit is alighted upon by the divine: saved, sanctified, and filled with the Holy Spirit.

There is no space here to discuss the full spectrum of the types of Christian experience and their formative capacities. Monastic asceticism, Baptistic freedom of conscience, Wesleyan holiness and perfection—these and countless other Christian spiritualities are experientially potent in shaping souls and charting out paths for intellectual inquiry. Bodies are touched, souls are healed, lives are restored, and the power of sin is overcome. Salvation in Christ thus transfigures our experiences of socialization and turns the fractures of intersectionality into resources for unique theological perspectives and opportunities.

4.4. The Fullness of the Spirit and the Life of the Mind

Although all Christians accept and even confess the person and work of the Spirit (in reciting the third article of the creed, for instance), a few conservative Protestant traditions do so only in word. In reality they are concerned that pneumatological overemphases will undermine biblical faith. On the other side, some pentecostal and charismatic overenthusiasts counter that "we walk by faith, not by sight" (2 Cor. 5:7), and thus perpetuate the perception that they are overly spiritually minded. These problems are partly the result of disjunctive understandings of the Spirit as opposed to Word, tradition, or reason.

It is now time to pull the threads of the quadrilateral together as we bring this first part of our book to a close. In the last four chapters we have discussed Scripture, tradition, reason, and experience, each in order. The attentive reader will have noticed that these have been accumulating discussions, rather than separate and distinct ones. This means that we have gradually understood how Scripture is mediated by tradition, how both Scripture and tradition shape Christian rationality and ways of thinking, and how Scripture, tradition, and reason are received experientially and formed through Christian conversion and discipleship. Throughout, we have also attempted to highlight that Scripture and the Spirit are not opposed, that tradition and charisma are two sides to one coin, and that reason and spirituality operate together. Christian experience is also possible only by and through the Holy Spirit: "in the one Spirit we were all baptized into one body—Jews or Greeks, slaves or free—and we were all made to drink of one Spirit" (1 Cor. 12:13). In short, the fullness of the Spirit is essential to the Christian life of the mind. The work of the Spirit is crucial to the task of Christian theologizing.

> *The Spirit-filled life renews and empowers the intellect.*

Jesus himself was Messiah as one anointed by the Spirit. In the book of Acts, Luke mentions "how God anointed Jesus of Nazareth with the Holy Spirit and with power; how he went about doing good and healing all who were oppressed by the devil, for God was with him" (Acts 10:38). This is consistent not just with the Gospels' portrait of Jesus' baptism involving the alighting of the Spirit upon him but also with how Jesus understood and presented, via appeal to the prophet Isaiah, his public ministry:

> The Spirit of the Lord is upon me,
> because he has anointed me
>   to bring good news to the poor.
> He has sent me to proclaim release to the captives
>   and recovery of sight to the blind,
>   to let the oppressed go free,
> to proclaim the year of the Lord's favor.
>   (Luke 4:18–19; cf. Isa. 61:1–2a)

In Luke's Gospel account, the Spirit's anointing of Jesus is exemplary of his anointing of Jesus' followers in his sequel, the book of Acts. Hearers also are urged by Jesus: "You shall love the Lord your God with all your heart, and with all your soul, and with all your strength, and *with all your mind*; and your neighbor as yourself" (Luke 10:27, emphasis added). The point to be noted is that for Luke, the Spirit-filled life involves, rather than abnegates, the renewal and empowerment of the intellect. The Christian life of the mind is spiritually enabled and enacted.

To be sure, to live in and by the Spirit is to be open to God's future, and this often is unimaginable by ourselves. The saving work of the Spirit provides a foretaste of the reign of God to come, as exemplified first and foremost in the life and ministry of Jesus. Surely, on our own accord, we will proclaim and work for our own kingdoms, to establish our own purposes. In that sense, the theological work inspired by the Spirit will be "abundantly far more than all we can ask or imagine" (Eph. 3:20b). There is thus a discontinuity between the Christian theological vision and mere human theological projections.

On the other hand, the incarnational and pentecostal narrative tells us that the mission of the triune God to save is focused on *this* world, its creatures in all their material brokenness, its history in all its fallenness, its nations and all their rebellion, and its human persons in all their sinfulness. Hence the Spirit speaks through the scriptural narratives of national fortunes and misfortunes (especially Israel's), and through the biblical accounts of the foibles of human sinners. The Spirit also works in and through the ups and downs of Christian traditions and somehow preserves the witness of the church in and through the vagaries of Christian churches. As Jesus promised: "I tell you, you are Peter, and on this rock I will build my church, and the gates of Hades will not prevail against it" (Matt. 16:18). It can also be affirmed that despite the development of human capacity to destroy ourselves and our earth, we have also developed medical cures, alleviated hunger, and developed enabling technologies, effectively enjoying the Spirit-enabled abilities of rational inquiry and pursuit. In sum, Christian theology can and ought to draw experientially from scriptural consideration, traditioned participation, and reasoned (and reasonable) deliberation.

Yet toward what end or ends? Ultimately, as already indicated, for the purposes of heralding the coming reign of God. Penultimately, however, theological reflection serves a multitude of other purposes. There is no such thing as theology in the abstract, in and for itself. Even contemplation of the divine is for various reasons, perhaps to understand better, to grasp more deeply the divine beauty and glory, or to love our neighbor more meaningfully. What are some of the purposes for theology? Part II will clarify such goals and objectives by focusing on the practices of theology: for persons, for the church, and for our work as young and aspiring theologians.

Discussion Questions

1. If one grows up as an orphan or without a parent, how might that impact one's understanding of God as father? How might Christian conversion redeem such life experiences?
2. How can we honor and respect the intersectional testimony of others while also recognizing that every dimension and domain of our lives have been corroded by sin? How does theology make redemption of such witness possible?
3. Can different Christian traditions be experienced as communicating charismatic gifts of the Spirit to the broader church ecumenical? If human experience is limited, even in Christ, how can we fully enjoy the gifts of our own church while also appreciating that of others?
4. Have you ever thought about Spirit-filled discipleship as including intellectual pursuits and the life of the mind? How does the Spirit use the Bible and Christian tradition in our lives to enable loving and serving God with all our minds?

For Further Reading

Alexander, Paul. *Signs and Wonders: Why Pentecostalism Is the World's Fastest Growing Faith*. San Francisco: Jossey-Bass, 2009.

Astley, Jeff, and Leslie J. Francis, eds. *Diversity and Intersectionality: Studies in Religion, Education, and Values*. Religion, Education, and Values 10. New York: Peter Lang, 2016.

Bantum, Brian. *The Death of Race: Building a New Christianity in a Racial World*. Minneapolis: Fortress Press, 2016.

Bevans, Stephen B. *Models of Contextual Theology*. Rev. and expanded ed. Maryknoll, NY: Orbis Books, 2013.

Gelpi, Donald L., SJ. *The Turn to Experience in Contemporary Theology*. New York: Paulist Press, 1994.

James, William. *The Varieties of Religious Experience: A Study in Human Nature*. 1902. Cambridge, MA: Harvard University Press, 1985. Many other eds.

Jones, Beth Felker. *Marks of His Wounds: Gender Politics and Bodily Resurrection*. Oxford: Oxford University Press, 2007.

Neumann, Peter D. *Pentecostal Experience: An Ecumenical Encounter*. Eugene, OR: Wipf & Stock, 2012.

Tanner, Kathryn. *Theories of Culture: A New Agenda for Theology*. Minneapolis: Fortress Press, 1997.

Thatcher, Adrian. *Theology and Families*. Malden, MA: Wiley-Blackwell, 2007.

Wariboko, Nimi. *The Pentecostal Principle: Ethical Methodology in New Spirit*. Grand Rapids: Wm. B. Eerdmans Publishing Co., 2011.

Yong, Amos. *The Bible, Disability, and the Church: A New Vision of the People of God*. Grand Rapids: Wm. B. Eerdmans Publishing Co., 2011.

———. *The Future of Evangelical Theology: Soundings from the Asian American Diaspora*. Downers Grove, IL: IVP Academic, 2014.

PART II

The Practices of Theology

5

Theology as Spiritual Practice

What Difference Does Theology Make in Our Personal Lives?

How do we get from the sources of theology to theological truth? "What is truth?" Pontius Pilate famously asked (John 18:38a). Jesus is the truth, Scripture indicates, but he is the truth by being the way and the life (John 14:6). Asking the questions about the truth of theology involves embarking on the way of Jesus and experiencing the life of the Spirit. Theological truths, therefore, are indissolubly interconnected with Christian practices. Herein, at this juncture, we shift from looking backward at the sources of theology to looking forward to the purposeful practices of theology.

Part II of this book examines three sets of Christian practices: that related to our personal daily lives (this chapter), that related to our ecclesial lives (chap. 6), and that related to the activities of young and aspiring theologians in colleges, universities, or seminaries (chap. 7). The final chapter in this book will disclose theology as a lifelong enterprise in and through the Spirit, springing out of an autobiographical perspective. Throughout this portion of the volume, the point is that theological reflection emerges out of life, responding to the exigencies of human life, and that we navigate these realities in and as people of the Spirit. Theology as thereby facilitated by, and as returning to inform, our practicing of Christian faith is a thoroughly spiritual endeavor.

This chapter looks at the spirituality of the (young) theologian, especially at how theology shapes our individual lives. We will discuss how theology enables our pursuit of God and things divine, how theology informs our relationship with others, and how theology predisposes us spiritually to the vagaries of daily existence. Theology for all individuals, laypersons or professional theologians, is part and parcel of the Christian sojourn. More precisely, theology is central to what it means to be led by the Spirit, and hence the final section considers the spirituality that relies on the promises of the gospel, of the kingdom and reign of God, that are coming and on their way.

5.1. Knowing and Loving God

Theology helps to clarify that God is and how we might relate to God. Theology cannot prove God in any mathematical or empirical sense. But theology can illuminate the ideas we imbibe from childhood or derive from life's passage that there is a Creator of all things, that there is a goal toward which the world is lurching and purpose for its creatures therein, and that the meaning and significance of our individual lives can best be understood within this wider story. If people of other, especially Eastern, faiths or spiritualities might not consider their lives in relationship to a personal and Creator God,

> *Hope appears, not as a proposition, but as an unasked-for gift. Theology attempts to understand how hope can be life-giving in the midst of severe circumstances.*

they are oftentimes nevertheless oriented toward some kind of transcendent hope, even a life after death of some sort. Christians, however, believe in faith that life is hopeful because it is cradled within the bosom of a loving God.

This is not to deny the pain, suffering, and profound tragedy that life in a sinful and fallen world brings. It is in this context that the Christian life of faith-seeking-understanding cannot be overstated. Such faith is not absolute: there is no rational guarantee that faith will persist through the challenges of life. And there are clear instances in which it boggles the mind to think that a personal and loving Deity would allow or create a world and its conditions producing the kind of anguish that we encounter. Not for no reason, there are those who are spiritual but not religious because they realize that they cannot survive without nurturing the human spirit. Yet they also find it impossible to embrace theism in its personalistic sense due to their perception of the reality of evil in a world purported to be good. There remains much that Christians can learn from such persons even if we remain steadfast in our faith.

This is in part because the Christian response of faith-seeking-understanding involves not just intellectualization but also comes about as an affective reception of and participation in divine grace (the encounter with the Spirit we saw in the previous chapter). Hope appears not as a proposition but as an unasked-for gift, and theology attempts to understand how such can be life-giving in the midst of severe circumstances. Theodicy, the question of how a benevolent God can allow such pain and suffering in the world, is answered ultimately less via scholarly treatises and more in human solidarity that sustains us through the tragedies and uncertainties of existence.

On the other side, unlike other animals, human beings are endowed with the curiosity and the capacity to wonder. There are moments, even prolonged occasions, when we find ourselves pondering and probing, not because we are paid professional theologians who find time to do so in the comforts of our studies, but because we observe a gorgeous creation, we hear a striking symphony, we are grasped by the beauty of a mathematical equation, or we are caught up in the profundity of a literary work. In the process, our thoughts are transfigured, leading us beyond ourselves. There is a fine line between finding traces of God in creation and beholding the beatific vision of the glorious triune God. Paul thus writes: "Ever since the creation of the world his eternal power and divine nature, invisible though they are, have been understood and seen through the things he has made" (Rom. 1:20). Theology enables us to ask better questions, to formulate better responses to our otherwise unutterable experiences of the sublime, and to attune our wonderment more and more appropriately.

As such, it should be obvious that theology and spirituality ought to be understood as two sides of the same coin. Our spiritual lives are oriented toward walking with God, and our theological understanding both guides that stroll and is enriched by it. Prayer is the two-way mode of communication between us and God, given language by Scripture, and exemplified within the tradition that precedes and sustains us. Prayer therefore presumes theology, an understanding of why God communicates with us, how that happens, and how to respond to God in that nexus. If our prayer is theologically funded, our theology is also prayerfully undertaken. Anselm (1033–1109), among the great medieval thinkers, wrote one of the most profound meditations of philosophical theology (*Proslogion*) about the existence of God from out of his praying. Prayerful spirituality bridges the spectrum between practical necessity on the one side and speculative wonder on the other side. Theology is needed for the full scope of ongoing prayer both in daily practice, as Paul commends, "Pray without ceasing"! (1 Thess. 5:17), and in contemplative meditation that extends our theological imagination and horizons.

It is true that one does not need a formal theological education to pray effectively or to enjoy ever deeper our friendship with God. But might not such a course of study provide additional resources for this trek? And what else does knowing God entail if not theological breadth and depth, the capacity to see our lives in all their ambiguities as still related to God, the ability to then also understand all things as the handiwork of the Creator, however murky the present world might appear? Growth of perspective in these spiritual things is decidedly theological. If we need words to understand ourselves, then extension of theological vocabulary and conceptualization leads to greater depth in Christian discipleship. It is not that one must have theological training to more fully experience and encounter the divine. But those of us who have been blessed with the opportunity for such studies get access to resources otherwise unavailable. Theology is vitalized therefore by spiritual practice, and vice versa, and these happen in the closets wherein we pray and across the full extent of the lives we lead.

5.2. Loving and Serving Our Neighbors

Theology is practiced therefore not only in our private spiritual devotion, but also in our public interactions. This organizational division of private and public is actually also interrelated. In this section we show how the practices of theology at work primarily in our relating to God also unfold in our interactions with others. If the love for God is related to but yet distinguishable from the love for neighbor, our discussion moves from the former to the latter, but now also clarifies their interconnectedness.

For all of its technicality and erudition (needed in certain contexts), in the end good, or at least better, theology is needed so we can lead good, at least better, lives. Thus Paul's theological treatise in Romans 1–11 offers theological argumentation about the sinfulness of creatures, righteousness in Christ, life in the Spirit, and the incorporation of Gentiles into the ancient covenant with Israel. Then Paul gives a very practical command: "I appeal to you therefore, brothers and sisters, by the mercies of God, to present your bodies as a living sacrifice, holy and acceptable to God, which is your spiritual worship" (Rom. 12:1). Romans 12–16 then includes admonitions to love one another, submit to authorities, live in holiness, esteem rather than judge others, edify rather than cause others to stumble, participate in the mission of God, and extend the presence, peace, and joy of Christ to our neighbors. Notice that a worshipful spirituality facilitates movement from more formal theological reflection about the work of God in Christ to more practical life interactions with others. Theology thus empowers such living with others in community, even as communal life generates (or ought to engender) better and better theology.

> *Theology invites more and more of the Spirit to be manifest in our lives.*

More pneumatologically, theology invites more and more of the Spirit to be manifest in our lives. Paul further reminds us that "the kingdom of God is not food and drink but righteousness and peace and joy in the Holy Spirit" (Rom. 14:17). We need more of the graces and fruits of the Spirit so that we can relate to others in love, joy, peace, patience, kindness, generosity, faithfulness, gentleness, self-control, cheerfulness, diligence, and compassion (Gal. 5:22–23; also Rom. 12:6–7). Theological reflection reiterates also that we need the power of the Spirit and the full expression of the charismatic gifts in order to build one another up and bear adequate witness to a watching world. The fruits and the gifts of the Spirit are not for ourselves but for our loving and serving others, enlivening their faith and drawing them, with us, into the divine presence and mystery. Theological understanding impresses upon us our need for the activity of the Holy Spirit, even as the bounty of the Spirit's fruits and the advent of the Spirit's gifts prompt (or ought to catalyze) further theological reflection and inquiry. The fact of the matter is that left to our own sinful devices, we end up living for ourselves rather than blessing others. This alienates and estranges human creatures rather than generates the community they want and need (without realizing it). Theology clarifies what hinders human communion even as it makes way for the divine Spirit to heal the fractures that keep people apart.

In the process, theological understanding makes possible not just our giving to and loving our neighbors but also our receiving and learning from them. Theology clearly teaches that all human creatures are made in the image of God (Gen. 1:27) and share in the divine breath (see §3.4 above). As such, Christian mission is not just to speak to others about God, as important and central as is such a task, but also to welcome others into the divine hospitality. As hosts of others in the divine presence, we are also mutual guests, receiving their gifts and testimonies. The Word and Son of God descended, via incarnation, as a guest of creation, even as the Spirit of God, poured out on all flesh, takes up residence as a guest in human hearts (cf. 1 Cor. 3:16; 6:19). Then similarly, as guests of our neighbors, we experience the divine gift of life through them. As Jesus taught through the parable of the Sheep and the Goats (Matt. 25:31–46), the former's salvation and the latter's damnation turned on the degree to which they entertained others in need. If the hungry are fed by us, if the thirst of others is quenched by us, if their nakedness is clothed by us, if the imprisoned are visited by us, and so forth, it is nevertheless we who experience God's redemption in and through their presence.

Theology thus orients us properly to others, chiefly our neighbors. Such reorientation also enables us to be transformed, to be saved and sanctified, by the triune God. Of course, again, it is not that only those with formal theological study are thus appropriately conformed, but we are beneficiaries of such occasions for theological reflection. Equally certain, "to whom much has been given, much will be required; and from one to whom much has been entrusted, even more will be demanded" (Luke 12:48b). So more will be expected from the theologically advanced, even as they (we!) ought to have greater resources out of which to love and serve.

5.3. Discerning the Spirit

If theology is spiritually invigorating and spirituality is theologically formative, then, as is being argued in this chapter, theology and the spiritual life are indivisibly intertwined. In this section, then, we will ask and answer, however preliminarily, three important questions about spiritual discernment at this intersection: (1) How do we discern God's will in and for our lives? (2) How do we discern the workings of the Holy Spirit in contrast to other spiritual stimuli? (3) How do we discern something to be of or from God in a world of many happenings? These are theological questions and invite theological responses that we shall see are interrelated.

Is it God's will for me to go to college, to date so and so, or to take out a car loan? How do we decide what God's will is for us in these and the innumerable other larger and smaller decisions that confront us over the course of life? Theology can be helpful here at least by clarifying that if we immerse ourselves in Scripture and the community of faith and ask the Holy Spirit to shape our hearts so that we can live in faithfulness to God according to the divine Word, then to some degree we can respond to any situation by acting prayerfully in faith. Our best estimation of the circumstances will be scripturally and communally considered. Are there guarantees that we might not be mistaken? No! But the promise of the gospel is that regardless of what has happened, nothing is beyond God's redemptive work. God can turn around any set of circumstances, even those actually harmful, for his good purposes (cf. Gen. 50:20; Rom. 8:28).

How can I discern the Holy Spirit from other spirits that might be operative in our world and in my life? How can I tell God's voice from the devil's? How do I tell the difference between the leading or prompting of the divine Spirit on one hand, and my own desires and aspirations on the other hand? At one level, one might need the charismatic gift of discernment of spirits (e.g., 1 Cor. 12:10). At another level, "every spirit that confesses that Jesus Christ has come in the flesh is from God, and every spirit that does not confess Jesus is not from God" (1 John 4:2b–3a). Yet at a third level and more generally speaking, the Spirit speaks through Scripture and the community of faith. This does not mean that every interpretation or personal application of Scripture is true, nor does it mean that every word of wisdom or word of knowledge given to us at charismatic prayer meetings is accurately heard (by others or by ourselves). It does mean that scriptural study and ecclesial discipleship foster our capacity to hearken to the divine voice and to attend to the Holy Spirit's nudges. It also means that we will, in time, gain greater and greater facility to recognize the voice and presence of the Good Shepherd (Jesus) and his Spirit, as well as develop more acuteness in identifying that of his enemy. If the latter is "the thief [that] comes only to steal and kill and destroy," Jesus also says: "My sheep hear my voice. I know them, and they follow me" (John 10:10a, 27). Spiritual discernment, in short, is attuned in both directions: to the Holy Spirit and not-so-holy spirits simultaneously.

> We do not have to say that everything that happens does so because God allows or causes it. We can say that whatever happens can be redeemed by God.

So, when can we be assured that any so-called *new thing* is a *good* thing, or is God's thing? How can we know when it is God who is present and active rather than mere creaturely goodwill or simply human ingenuity? Is everything that happens divinely ordained in some way, as some theologies might say? What about creaturely freedom to enact good things: are these providentially achieved as well? Some might find comfort in a strict divine determinism that understands every event as intended by God, whether for salvation or damnation (according to one interpretation of Rom. 9). But it is arguably just as effective, if not more so, to view history in light of God's reign embodied in and proclaimed by Jesus, without linking every happenstance to God's specific will. We do not need to say that things happen because God allows or causes their occurrence. Yet we can say that whatever happens can be redeemed by God and that those events consistent with the character of the divine kingdom revealed in Jesus' life and teachings assist in our own heralding the reign of God. Are all new things God's things? If signs of the reign of God are evidenced, yes! If these are absent, we might still pray and work more fervently in that situation so that the Spirit might interrupt and the presence of Christ be made more tangible. In short, theology can help discern the new thing God is doing precisely by empowering our response to whatever is happening.

On the one hand, these are difficult questions, and the brief responses above are certainly too self-assured. On the other hand, what is clear is that these are all deeply theological kinds of issues. Life's journey, in other words, necessarily involves theology, whether or not we ever get the chance to pursue theological education more formally. Even more unarguably, such theological capacity and wisdom cannot but emerge over time, even when formal study is involved. For Christians, then, theology is a lifelong companion, even if one never encounters the word or concept!

5.4. Eschatological Rationality

Since theology is a lifelong undertaking, this chapter concludes with the invitation to explore and embrace what we might call an eschatological imagination or form of reasoning. *Eschaton*, from the Greek, usually refers to the last things or the events at the end of time. But alternatively, the *eschaton* also refers to teachings of Jesus about the coming kingdom of God, as in the message of the Sermon on the Mount. Such an eschatological rationality, hence, is shown in and anticipates the divine reign lived out and preached by Jesus. The eschatological reality I am thinking about here is therefore *not* about the end-times ideas of Tim LaHaye and other such prognosticators of the second coming. Instead, eschatological hope concerns the coming kingdom of heaven, initially embodied in the person of Christ, with its basic contours preserved in the apostolic message. The eschatological also refers to the present reality of the Spirit's pentecostal work as that which makes real aspects of this divine message even while nurturing a longing in us for its full actualization in God's appointed future. In that sense, eschatological reality concerns both the now (urgently) and the not-yet (secondarily).

> We can admit that, for now, we know only in part, while yearning for the day that will reveal the fullness of God's glory.

Christian spirituality, as discussed in this chapter, has personal and interrelational dimensions. Both are fundamentally theological in that theological ideas undergird the spiritual quest even as they expand the theological horizons. Christian spirituality is hence dynamic rather than static, historically fluid rather than abiding in any eternal-now. Insofar as the Spirit of Pentecost is also the Spirit poured out "in the last days" (Acts 2:17a), in the present era the pentecostal breath of God also is a harbinger of the eschatological reign to come. As such, eschatological rationality is also pneumatological as the Pentecost Spirit bridges creation's present and God's future.

Christian eschatological and pneumatological spirituality lives in the present in anticipation of the divine reign. The author of the First Letter to John writes thus: "What we will be has not yet been revealed. What we do know is this: when he is revealed, we will be like him, for we will see him as he is" (1 John 3:2). Herein faith-seeking-understanding is expressed in christological and eschatological terms. We know Christ only in part, but one day we shall know him fully: this is the christological promise. We know Christ only in part, but one day we shall know him more completely: this is the eschatological hope. Christian spirituality that is theologically informed in this way enables our embrace of and participation in this eschatological message. We acknowledge the partiality of what we know in the present yet yearn for the full revelation of Jesus rather than being paralyzed by skepticism or agnosticism. It is precisely the hope of more fully knowing, and of being more fully known, that compels the theological venture.

The Pauline tradition says that in Christ, "you also, when you had heard the word of truth, the gospel of your salvation, and had believed in him, were marked with the seal of the promised Holy Spirit; this is the pledge of our inheritance toward redemption as God's own people, to the praise of his glory" (Eph. 1:13–14; cf. 2 Cor. 1:22; 5:5). The Spirit is thus the deposit or earnest divine pledge that God's covenant people will realize the promised salvation. Having thus had a foretaste of this divine love in and through the Spirit (Rom. 5:5; Col. 1:8), the people of God continue to ask and pray that they "may be filled with the knowledge of God's will in all spiritual wisdom and understanding, so that you may lead lives worthy of the Lord, fully pleasing to him, as you bear fruit in every good work and as you grow in the knowledge of God" (Col. 1:9b–10). The eschatological hope is the vision of Jesus Christ as "the image of the invisible God, the firstborn of all creation; for in him all things in heaven and on earth were created, things visible and invisible, whether thrones or dominions or rulers or powers—all things have been created through him and for him. He himself is before all things, and in him all things hold together. He is the head of the body, the church; he is the beginning, the firstborn from the dead, so that he might come to have first place in everything" (Col. 1:15–18).

The truth of God manifest in Jesus of Nazareth will come into full and glorious view eschatologically (now and later). Such an eschatological rationality and spirituality thus persevere despite the partial perspective that clouds human knowledge during this present era. There is an ongoing pressing into the knowledge of God revealed in Jesus without ever exhausting what can be known. Thus one can grow in intimacy with the divine by the Spirit but always deepen in intensity. Similarly, in and by the Spirit one can give oneself away in love and service to God and neighbor without exhausting one's capacities. One lifetime is insufficient to plumb the depths of Scripture, to fathom the riches of Christian traditions, to be excited by the wonder and curiosity of the remarkable human brain, and to experience fully the love of God in Christ by the Spirit.

This does not mean that the eschatological rationality and logic persist only in ignorance. The way, truth, and life of Jesus are sure in faith, even if open to greater clarification. What we come to realize not only in our heads and minds but also in the depths of our creaturely hearts and in the relationships forged by human hands is "the depth of the riches and wisdom and knowledge of God! How unsearchable are his judgments and how inscrutable his ways!" (Rom. 11:33). Yet such unsearchability and inscrutability do not hamper the spiritual life but inspire such in and through the mundane yet grace-filled reality of Christian existence.

Discussion Questions

1. In what ways can you imagine your theological study playing a role in your devotional life or in your spiritual explorations?
2. Can you envision how theological reflection might inspire and elevate to a higher level your relationships with family and friends or your interactions with strangers?
3. What is God's will for your life? How have your experiences so far opened up a range of possible theologically informed responses to this question?
4. Is always growing in love and increasing in knowledge of God, forever and ever, tiring or energizing for your spirituality? Why?

For Further Reading

Bruner, Frederick Dale, and William Hordern. *The Holy Spirit: Shy Member of the Trinity*. Minneapolis: Augsburg Fortress, 1984.

Cartledge, Mark J. *Encountering the Spirit: The Charismatic Tradition*. Maryknoll, NY: Orbis Books, 2007.

Chan, Simon. *Spiritual Theology: A Systematic Study of the Christian Life*. Downers Grove, IL: IVP Academic, 1998.

Clark, David K. *To Know and Love God: Method for Theology*. Wheaton, IL: Crossway, 2003.

Fiand, Barbara. *Come, Drink Deep of Living Waters: Faith Seeking Understanding in the 21st Century*. New York: Crossroad, 2016.

Jones, Scott J. *The Evangelistic Love of God & Neighbor: A Theology of Witness & Discipleship*. Nashville: Abingdon Press, 2005.

Navonne, John. *Toward a Theology of Beauty*. Collegeville, MN: Liturgical Press, 1996.

Nouwen, Henri. *Discernment: Reading the Signs of Daily Life*. New York: Harper, 2013.

Packer, J. I. *Knowing God*. Downers Grove, IL: InterVarsity Press, 1973.

Rahner, Karl. *Theological Investigations*. Vol. 14, *Experience of the Spirit, Source of Theology*. New York: Seabury, 1979.

Rausch, Thomas. *Eschatology, Liturgy, and Christology: Toward Recovering an Eschatological Imagination*. Collegeville, MN: Michael Glazier, 2012.

Willard, Dallas. *The Spirit of the Disciplines: Understanding How God Changes Lives*. New York: HarperOne, 1999.

Yong, Amos. *Hospitality and the Other: Pentecost, Christian Practices, and the Neighbor*. Faith Meets Faith Series. Maryknoll, NY: Orbis Books, 2008.

6

Theology as Ecclesial Practice

By, for, and through the Church

The preceding chapter looked at the practices of theology from the perspective of the individual as person. Thus we considered primarily the devotional and intersubjective dimensions of theology as spiritual practice. Now we turn to look at the practices of theology in relationship to the church. Arguably, we could have proceeded in reverse direction, first examining theology's ecclesial practices that in turn shape how we consider theology's spiritual practices. Obviously each informs the other: our personal spiritualities are ecclesially embedded since they are undertaken by members of the body of Christ and participants in the fellowship of the Spirit. Hence Christian spirituality has an ecclesial shape. The foregoing thus needs to be reconsidered in the present discussion even as the eschatological rationality presented above will shape that which is to come.

We therefore explore the broader ecclesial dimension of our theological efforts by drawing on the historic (Nicene) definition of the marks of the church as one, holy, catholic (worldwide), and apostolic. Thus the four sections of this chapter will consider how theology (1) enables working out the church's identity and toward doctrinal unity, (2) shapes the church's life of holiness, (3) sustains the thriving of the global church in its diversity, and (4) empowers a pluriform mission (the word "apostolic" referring to "one who is sent") in multiple spheres. These are interrelated aspects of the people of God as a pentecostal phenomenon even as they exist in some tension. They underscore the Spirit's role of ushering in the divine reign and shaping the church as an eschatological reality. There are certainly many other ecclesial purposes for theology that we will not be touching on here. Building on

77

chapter 2 above, our goal is to be suggestive and overarching about the ecclesial practices of theology, not to be all-inclusive and too detailed.

Here we shall see that the church therefore also is a living and organic
body, catalyzed by the Spirit's eschatological work. In that sense the church,
constituted by its members (us) and their (our) practices, foreshadows and
anticipates the divine reign, giving way to that coming reality. It will be within
this context, then, that we can better understand our own formal theological
education and formation, the focused discussion of the next chapter. Our
practices as theological students (chaps. 7–8) can be better comprehended as
intrinsic to, rather than apart from, our participation in the new and restored
Israel as the church of God.

6.1. The Church as One: Dogmatic Identity and Ecclesial Unity

We have already seen in chapter 2 that the one church over the last two
millennia has been developed by many traditions, has produced an ecumenical set of creeds and also multiple later confessions and doctrinal statements
of faith (especially in the Protestant world), and is now constituted globally
through a bewildering diversity of languages and cultures. Our focus in that
discussion was to observe how these various traditions of the church also
could be received as resources for the theological task, particularly when we
realize the role of the Spirit in guiding the development of the church's self-
understanding over space and time. In this section, however, the question is
how theology shapes the practices of the church understood as one, a question clearly complicated by the church's global plurality. The suggestion here
is that theology enables appreciation, understanding, and collaborative effort
even amid doctrinal diversity. To see this, let us assess the church's doctrinal
differences by observing, as with the scriptural tradition in the first chapter,
the worlds *behind, within,* and *in front of* ecclesial creeds and confessions.

Theological training helps us *appreciate* ecclesial doctrinal commitments
first by helping us to grasp the historical factors that have led to the generation of creedal or confessional statements to begin with. People don't just sit
down one day to craft a theological statement that then turns into a dogmatic
set of commitments. Rather, there are historical realities that prompt theological questions, and eventually a consensus is argued for, even if such is not
achieved either immediately or subsequently (as should be obvious since it
is often argumentation that prompts confessional articulation to begin with).
In this respect, the shift from theological to doctrinal understanding seeks to
demarcate what ought to be promoted and why, which in turn is designed to
clarify commitments and to exclude those who hold counterpositions. In this
respect, there is an ecclesial politics that produces dogmas and creates, at least

in theory, "insiders" and "outsiders." In many cases it is arguable whether there are actually any who hold the "outsider" position or whether those proponents have more nuanced perspectives or come to believe otherwise, perhaps even through the process of disputation. Theological consideration enables us to realize what historical forces are behind doctrinal divisions and to situate these creeds and statements in these various contexts.

> *Theological analysis helps us both understand the positive claims of creeds and confessions, but also where they reflect the mystery of God by reminding us of what we can't know.*

Theological study also provides us with the tools to *understand* ecclesial doctrinal differences, especially the capacity to analyze the nature of such confessions. If biblical hermeneutical approaches to the scriptural text lift up their literary, narrative, and intertextual features, theological hermeneutics illuminates what creeds and doctrinal statements are affirming and what they are denying. For instance, the Chalcedonian Creed (451) regarding the person of Christ declares him as

> one and the same Son, our Lord Jesus Christ, the same perfect in Godhead [against those who questioned the divine nature] and also perfect in manhood [here countering questions on the other side]; truly God and truly man, of a reasonable soul and body [here against what was taught by Apollinarus, bishop of Laodicea/Latakia in Syria]; consubstantial with the Father according to the Godhead, and consubstantial with us according to the Manhood [here extending what the Nicene confession says about the Son]; in all things like unto us, without sin; begotten before all ages of the Father according to the Godhead [here continuing to oppose the earlier heresy of Arianism], and in these latter days, for us and for our salvation, born of the Virgin Mary, the Mother of God [here granting what was said also by Nestorius, patriarch of Constantinople, 428–431], according to the Manhood; one and the same Christ, Son, Lord, only begotten, to be acknowledged in two natures [but here resisting other claims of Nestorius], inconfusedly, unchangeably, indivisibly, inseparably. . . .

Theological analysis thus opens up the historical disputes behind the text. More importantly, the paradox of the incarnation is affirmed not only by declaring what we believe in and know, but also by clarifying what we do not understand. So the last four terms, "inconfusedly, unchangeably, indivisibly, inseparably," are not positive statements but negative descriptions. They indicate how Jesus in one person in two natures is *not* to be understood, as opposed to saying what this means. Theological analysis of this confession thus helps us understand how the creed makes concrete claims but also how it preserves elements of the mystery of revelation by using conceptualities available to its drafters in their place and time.

This leads, third, to the proposal that theological work also *enables collaborative efforts* that build on and reappropriate prior achievements. Doctrinal statements, including creeds and confessions of all sorts, are not just for the purposes of theological information but also provide a common platform for Christian practice. We do not just believe such documents in our heads but especially allow the convictions expressed therein to guide our work. This is the world *in front of* the creedal or confessional statement and invites a future for those who can appreciate its historicity, understand what it affirms and what it leaves open, and can then move forward. What results might not be an overturning of the confession later but its deeper comprehension via the process of practical reception. Our capacity to work together amid the variety of confessional frames that inform our theological identities itself gives meaning to those statements, extended significance perhaps unanticipated by their original framers. In this respect, the church's unity is negotiated practically on this side of the eschaton, rather than through achieving doctrinal unanimity and uniformity.

None of this is intended to say that there might not be moments when doctrinal disagreements are serious enough to require the parting of ways. That is part of the purpose of achieving doctrinal understanding. However, the other part just as important to take away is that doctrinal confessions are historically debated and argued about not just at the point of their initial formulation but in their reception by later generations of believers in different contexts. Such might lead to new creedal articulations for different times and purposes, and such collaborative activities are possible for those who are theologically informed and resourced. These might not negate their predecessors but would enrich the heritage and self-understanding of the church. Such is part of the work of the church as an eschatological reality: always reforming as needed and always being renewed by the Holy Spirit even in its theological self-understanding in anticipating the fullness of truth to be revealed in the coming age.

6.2. The Church as Holy: The Social Distinctiveness of the Ecclesia

If the doctrinal unity of the church has eschatological shape, its ongoing reception and renewal are part of the collaborative outworking of its many members. This connects to the understanding of the church as holy, set apart

as the body of Christ, and purified to be the bride of the Lamb in that eschatological banquet. The church is therefore fully holy as the betrothed, but still
being made holy during this eschatological time. How does theology inform
the practices of a church that is set apart
from the world yet in the world?

> *The love of God is manifest,*
> *not just as we enable our*
> *neighbors' individual welfare,*
> *but also as we confront their*
> *collective plight and fortunes.*

Here our objective for ecclesial practice is to understand the implications of
the notion that the church is holy and set
apart for God's good and final purposes.
At least three trajectories of practical
consequences are possible. First, the
church as the body of Christ and the communion of the Holy Spirit is institutionally, organizationally, liturgically, and otherwise always historical. The
church is called to be the people of a covenant God, not to be the synagogue,
the mosque, or the temple. The church is called to be those gathered around
the Eucharist, or Lord's Supper, and around the preaching of the Word, not to
be a club, a social gathering, a welfare site, or a political office, even if there are
aspects of the church's ministry that might touch on matters in these realms.
The point is that the church is called "to the apostles' teaching and fellowship, to the breaking of bread and the prayers" (Acts 2:42). The church is first
and foremost God-centered, and theology ought to support and strengthen
this central vocation. In living out this calling, however, the church is a fully
public manifestation. The church's God-centeredness will be distinctive and
countercultural precisely because these other realms, entities, and realities are
not similarly oriented and constituted. In short, even the church's divine focus
finds full and expanded significance only in its public situatedness.

Yet the church as holy is also called to live out the divinely ordained patterns for human creatures and the world. As such, part of the church's being
made holy involves the ways in which it bears witness to the world's lack of
holiness and seeks to reform and purify these realities. Here, second, public
theological presence leads to socioeconomic theological performance. The
love of God is intertwined with the love of neighbor, not just as we enable our
neighbors' individual welfare but also as we confront their collective plight
and fortunes. The preceding chapter traced out the theological underpin-
nings and implications for loving our neighbors at an interpersonal level; here
we infer the consequences at the ecclesial level. Rather than being abstractly
theological, ecclesial love for neighbor is thoroughly ethical, practical, and
structural. Take, for instance, James's claim: "Religion that is pure and unde-
filed before God, the Father, is this: to care for orphans and widows in their
distress, and to keep oneself unstained by the world" (Jas. 1:27). Caring
for orphans and widows is shaped by cultural conventions, involves social

structures, and has economic dimensions. This Jamesian principle is but an extension of the Old Testament prophets' concern that Israel care for the most vulnerable members of society: the migrants, the poor, and the sick or impaired. Sure, the church at one level ought to set up soup kitchens and rescue missions to feed the hungry and shelter the homeless, ought to establish visiting teams to visit those in jail or prison, and ought to build hospitals, retirement homes, and orphanages, and the like. These embody the practical truths related to the church being made holy and transformed into the image of Christ.

Yet at another level the church, in and through its members, organizations, and institutions (variously manifest in the sociopolitical structures in place around the world), ought also to prevail upon leaders to enact just laws to protect the marginalized members of society and to enhance the possibility of their flourishing. How are refugees, exiles, and forced migrants, for instance, treated in any society? How might the experiences of these groups of people be doubly, triply, or quadruply jeopardized by intersectional factors (see §4.2 above)? What kinds of laws are in place? How ought the church to engage with public governments, to the degree possible (in some cases, such influence is tangential if not altogether unmanageable), in order to ensure that greater justice prevails on behalf of these most voiceless in society? Here socioeconomic theology blends into political theology proper: the implications of Christian faith for public policy, social governance, and political practice. The sanctification of Christian churches in whatever societies, nations, or regions of the world cannot be isolated from the justness—or lack thereof—of their broader stances and activities. Practicing ecclesial holiness must be worked out in these social, economic, and political realms.

These are the practical demands for working out the church's holiness in the world since sanctification follows from justification. In the Christian doctrine of personal salvation, the justification of sinners involves our being declared to be in right standing with God, while our sanctification involves the making righteous of our lives and deeds. Ecclesially, however, the church that is declared holy nevertheless ought to live and work as such, and the latter occurs in the public square. Hence the church's countercultural identity does not insulate its members from public effort but more starkly highlights whether the church practices what is preached. In other words, the truth of the church's holiness and right standing before God involves making right our standing with others and our relating to others. Jesus admonished: "When you are offering your gift at the altar, if you remember that your brother or sister has something against you, leave your gift there before the altar and go; first be reconciled to your brother or sister, and then come and offer your gift" (Matt. 5:23–24). Reconciliation with our neighbor is central to walking with the God of Jesus Christ. So holiness is expressed, interpersonally and socioecclesially, as part and parcel of the theological witness of the holy people of God.

6.3. The Church as Catholic:
Global Cultures and Ecclesial Witness

From Pentecost onward, it should go without saying (although some of this was said in §2.3 above), the church has been a multicultural reality. This multiculturality is manifest in and through the church's distinctive tongues, which in turn resist homogeneity of language or uniformity of practices. Thus, the apocalyptic vision in the book of Revelation of the eschatological people of God is described as a "great multitude that no one could count, from every nation, from all tribes and peoples and languages" (Rev. 7:9). But what are the practical implications of this conviction that the church's catholicity is multicultural?

For one thing, the church's liturgy will be conducted in the vernacular and will be manifest in culturally specific forms relative to congregational and parish sites. Here we are talking not only of musical instrumentation (for the majority that are not a cappella), which is culturally relative, but also of organizational form, aesthetic design, and architectural structure, among other culturally contextual dimensions of incarnational and pentecostal communities of worship. Making worship fit within new or different cultures involves reappropriation of cultural resources, and it is theological work to discern when such accommodation remains a faithful expression of Christian faith and practice. The church's catholicity, in short, demands translation of the gospel across cultures, and continuously so since cultures themselves are not static entities.

But here is where theological discussion and debate get convoluted, as the means of argumentation conducted in other languages involves nuances not easily translatable across cultures. The theology of the churches that embraced the conciliar traditions of the first millennium has been shaped by Platonic philosophical modes of thinking. Then the Latin West in particular included Aristotelian concepts through Aquinas and other scholastics (see §3.1 above). In contrast, churches in South Asia think also in Brahmanic and Vedic (Hindu) terms, while those in East Asia are steeped in Daoist, Buddhist, and Confucian thought forms. Hence the multicultural church already draws on a variety of philosophical systems and methods to shape its reflection on the truth of the gospel. It is not always easy to untangle the material content of Christian teaching from its mental forms when these are conducted in and through many languages. Theology is thus central to the church's catholicity, not least as the church works out the implications of its self-understanding in different cultural places and linguistic times.

The preceding alerts us to the fact that the church's multiculturality involves an encounter with people of other religions and faiths. In some contexts, it is clear that Eastern, especially East Asian, traditions are philosophical and not religious, at least not in any conventional theistic sense. Yet in the main, the three Chinese traditions (Daoism, Confucianism, and Buddhism) are recognized to have religious, certainly spiritual, elements. Hinduism is also a form of theism even if it is not strictly monotheistic. To the degree that the many cultures of the world are interrelated with the world's religious traditions, to that same degree the nature of the church's catholicity has to be understood alongside of, but yet as interfacing with, the great religious and wisdom traditions of the world. Also, indigenous cultures are now surging and will need to be factored in.

> *The church's catholicity stands alongside, but also interfaces with, the world's great traditions of religious wisdom.*

The catholicity of the church thus takes theological practice. Here we are not just talking about how to distinguish Christian teachings from beliefs of other religions since that is, as such, easy enough to catalog. But how can we compare them? How can we discern and decide between them? The work of interreligious apologetics is to clarify convictions in relationship to those in other faiths and to defend them when under questioning. Where contextually appropriate, interreligious apologetics also mounts critical questions and dialogical counterquestions. The catholicity of the church remains an unfinished hope to the degree that the members of Christ's body do not develop appropriate skills to engage with people of other faith traditions in the public square. Such interactions can only be edifying (even when they do not result in mass conversions to Christian faith) if conducted with theological skill and maturity.

Yet interreligious exchange involves not just argumentation but also sociality. The practices of ecclesial catholicity, in other words, require proficiencies in living as culturally and religiously distinct in a pluralistic world on the one hand and yet in ways that promote the common good on the other hand. In short, catholic faith has interreligious dimensions so that the practices of catholicity involve living together amid our differences and working together with these varying commitments. If in our globalizing world the public square is increasingly multicultural and multireligious, then the practices of world Christianity must be able to galvanize partners to work for the common good in the social, economic, and political spheres (§6.2 immediately above). Achieving justice and righteousness at the social, national, and international levels requires cooperation with all people of goodwill. Such work inevitably involves those of other languages, cultures, and religious convictions. Theological wisdom is essential to navigating these public and pluralistic currents since interaction will often impact self-understanding. Simultaneously, Christian catholicity in these interfaces also will have their immeasurable impact, perhaps extending ecclesial unity and holiness in unforeseeable ways.

> *Why insulate ourselves from the world's cultural-religious diversity? There is no getting away from the theological challenges and opportunities before us.*

Needless to say, some might consider such interfaith engagement and especially cooperation to be fraught with risks and prefer a more cautious and reserved posture. Can we keep our children from making friends who are not like them, however, or dictate where they go to school, who they work with in their places of employment, or who their neighbors are in the next-door apartment? Can we prevent our grandchildren from marrying those from other cultures, or even other faith traditions? Navigating these realities is decidedly theological. The deeper question is also equally theological: why insulate ourselves from the world's cultural-religious diversity in the first place? There is no getting away from the theological challenges and opportunities before us. Ecclesially and practically speaking, however (which is the focus in this chapter), such deliberation and its related activities are part and parcel of what it means to express Christian faith and discipleship in a pluralistic and changing world.

6.4. The Church as Apostolic: The Many Tongues of the Spirit's Mission

Apostolicity concerns the church's links to the message that Jesus handed to his disciples, the twelve apostles, to proclaim and enact. In that respect, to be apostolic means, in some significant sense, holding fast to the teachings of the apostles, recorded in the writings of the New Testament. Apostolicity in a technical sense, however, also means just *being sent*: the disciples were so commissioned: "Go therefore and make disciples of all nations, baptizing them in the name of the Father and of the Son and of the Holy Spirit, and teaching them to obey everything that I have commanded you" (Matt. 28:19–20a). In that vein, the apostolicity of the church means also that those of every later generation, including you and me, are likewise called to carry out this primordial task of inviting and making disciples of Jesus.

Considerations of the church as one, holy, and catholic are leading us relentlessly to apostolicity. We can understand the Spirit's making the church united, holy, and catholic as part of its apostolic mandate and mission. If the nature of the church is tied in with its witness and mission—as indicated in the preceding discussions, especially about the church's holiness and catholicity—then there is finally no separating these four elements of the church. To believe in the church as one, holy, and catholic is to be on an apostolic mission as the church. The theology of and about the church (ecclesiology, more technically) therefore turns on the church's ministerial and missionary practices. What the church does tells us more about what the church is than what the church says about itself. Jesus himself said to the apostles: "I give you a new commandment, that you love one another. Just as I have loved you, you also should love one another. By this everyone will know that you are my disciples, if you have love for one another" (John 13:34–35).

> *Theology supports and is transformed by the church's mission.*

Pulling the threads of this and even the preceding chapter together, then, we recognize that theology supports and is transformed by the practicalities of the church's mission. Such missionary endeavors of course include personal witnessing (included in especially §5.2) and evangelistic proclamation. These lead to the establishment of congregations (and the transformation of parish communities for those more historically rooted), in and through which the church's mission to society and the public square are organized and authorized. If the members of the apostolic community "had all things in common" (Acts 2:44b), as shown in selling what they had in order to care for the needier in their midst, it was in that context that "day by day the Lord added to their number those who were being saved" (Acts 2:47). The point is that the church's mission, from the start, involved organizational and economic elements, with real public consequences. "Church growth" and multiplication in effect took care of themselves in that milieu.

There is one more dimension to the church's mission that we ought to consider theologically: the cosmic dimensions of ecclesial catholicity. If the church is global or worldwide, then it is universal in the terrestrial sense. Yet the Scriptures themselves indicate that God's salvific plans are not merely human but also cosmic in their horizons: "The creation was subjected to futility, not of its own will but by the will of the one who subjected it, in hope that the creation itself will be set free from its bondage to decay and will obtain the freedom of the glory of the children of God. We know that the whole creation has been groaning in labor pains until now; and not only the creation, but we ourselves, who have the first fruits of the Spirit, groan inwardly while we wait for adoption, the redemption of our bodies" (Rom. 8:20–23). In part for this reason, then, "the Spirit helps us in our weakness; for we do not know how to pray as we ought, but that very Spirit intercedes with sighs too deep for words" (Rom. 8:26). Since the Spirit is concerned about the creation, which includes the natural environment and the ecosphere, then those so filled also ought to pray for and act toward its renewal. Hence there is an ecological and cosmic vista to the apostolic mission of the church.

Some might demur that Christian witness ought to focus on the salvation of human souls and not the material earth and nonhuman creatures since, in the end, "the heavens will be set ablaze and dissolved, and the elements will melt with fire" (2 Pet. 3:12b). This is of course also a position justified from the surface of the scriptural text. So the questions are inevitably theological: How ought we to understand these biblical references? What are their implications for our lives in particular and for the church's witness and mission more broadly understood? Theological study and formation are required to engage such questions and anticipate their practical effects as they directly implicate Christian ministry and mission. The descent of the new heavens upon a renovated earth invites further consideration of a theology of the re-created environment. This task needs to inform, and be informed by, mission practices related to sustainable ecological engagement.

The argument in this chapter is an extension of the previous one: theology is important for personal discipleship and ecclesial mission, and Christian life and church practice also return to inspire theological reflection. We do theology so that we can live more rightly, love more deeply, and serve more potently, even as our living, loving, and serving as followers of Jesus require ongoing theological examination. There are surely many other purposes for which ecclesial practice can and ought to be theologically compelled. Our task in this chapter, however, is to provide only glimpses of the interrelationship between theology and practice, not to conclude a comprehensive discussion. The hope is that the foregoing sketches will be sufficient for extrapolation into other contexts, tasks, and purposes.

More importantly, given the eschatological character of the church's being transformed in unity, holiness, and catholicity, we ought to press forward in inquiring faith, believing that the apostolic truth will prevail. All truth is God's truth: it is an essential part of the spiritual search and the church's vocation to witness, however partially and fallibly, to the truth that it understands. This is done with the expectation that when and after "the Spirit of truth comes, he will guide you into all the truth" (John 16:13), especially the fullness of the truth in the person of Jesus. Christian disciples' faithfulness is expressed and manifest in mission so that all theology is missional or missiological in some respect, even as all missionary engagement and Christian witness are theologically informed and ecclesially carried.

Discussion Questions

1. Is a new ecumenical creed possible today given the many cultures and languages of contemporary world Christianity? Might such a confession of unity be distillable instead from the church's missionary practices? How so?
2. What are the basic theological elements that connect the holiness of the church with Christian social, economic, and political engagement? How might such endeavors animate or sidetrack the church?
3. How is the catholicity of the church multicultural? What is the implication of such for interfaith interactions or for our attitudes and approaches to people of other faiths? What are the limits, if any, to our collaboration with religious others in the public square?
4. How else might we develop a theology of care for the environment? Can our recycling efforts, for instance, be understood as an extension of the apostolic message? What are other implications of the church's apostolicity in this regard, if any?

For Further Reading

Bosch, David Jacobus. *Transforming Mission: Paradigm Shifts in Theology of Mission.* Maryknoll, NY: Orbis Books, 1991.

Brunner, Daniel L., Jennifer L. Butler, and A. J. Swoboda. *Introducing Evangelical Ecotheology: Foundations in Scripture, Theology, History, and Praxis.* Grand Rapids: Baker Academic, 2014.

Lodahl, Michael, and April Cordero Maskiewicz. *Renewal in Love: Living Holy Lives in God's Good Creation.* Kansas City, MO: Beacon Hill, 2014.

Lord, Andy. *Network Church: A Pentecostal Ecclesiology Shaped by Mission.* Global Pentecostal and Charismatic Studies 11. Leiden: Brill, 2012.

Myers, Bryant L. *Engaging Globalization: The Poor, Christian Mission, and Our Hyperconnected World.* Grand Rapids: Baker Academic, 2017.

Newbigin, Lesslie. *The Gospel in a Pluralist Society.* Grand Rapids: Wm. B. Eerdmans Publishing Co., 1989.

Oord, Thomas Jay, and Michael Lodahl. *Relational Holiness: Responding to the Call to Love.* Kansas City, MO: Beacon Hill Press, 2011.

Pasquale, Michael, and Nathan L. K. Bierma. *Every Tribe and Tongue: A Biblical Vision for Language in Society.* Eugene, OR: Wipf & Stock, 2011.

Sanneh, Lamin O. *Translating the Message: The Missionary Impact on Culture.* 2nd ed. Maryknoll, NY: Orbis Books, 2009.

Sullivan, Francis Aloysius. *The Church We Believe In: One, Holy, Catholic, and Apostolic.* New York: Paulist Press, 1988.

Yong, Amos. *In the Days of Caesar: Pentecostalism and Political Theology.* Grand Rapids: Wm. B. Eerdmans Publishing Co., 2010.

———. *The Missiological Spirit: Christian Mission Theology for the Third Millennium Global Context.* Eugene, OR: Cascade Books, 2014.

7

Theology as Scholarly Practice

Researching, Writing, and Studying Theology

S
o far in this second part of the book, we have focused on theological practices. Theological ideas have consequences, even
as such ideas usually derive from existing practical realities.
Our discussion thus far has been on our personal lives as believing Christians
(chap. 5) and on our collective lives in the church as disciples of Jesus Christ
(chap. 6). In this chapter we turn more directly to the practices of theology
that are prevalent in the immediate contexts wherein most readers of this
book might find themselves: the college or university classroom.

This chapter provides some concrete suggestions to young (first-year) and
aspiring theologians, particularly at the undergraduate level (but also for
first-year seminarians without formal theological background in their prior
studies). We will start with the initial theological assignments, discuss the
term-long research paper, address the central question of faith integration
that permeates curricular and pedagogical discussions in Christian higher
education, and conclude with a consideration of theological writing as a spiritual discipline in its own right. The primary purpose is to consider the habits and disciplines, learning-related and spiritual, that undergird and propel
success as theological students. If theology has practical implications and
consequences, then our goal here is to trace these out in the course of our
theological studies.

Part of the thesis to be presented in the next few pages extends a thread
already woven in this book regarding the spirituality of theological education.
We might study theology to be more spiritual or to be more adept spiritually.
But we might also need to foster spiritual practices that can enable us to be

better theologians. This is what it means to say that theological beliefs and practices are interrelated, particularly by and through the work of the Holy Spirit, the point of part II of this book. The next and final chapter will complete the argument for this case.

7.1. The Initial Contexts of (Undergraduate) Theologizing

How might one survive, even succeed with high marks or grades, in one's first theology course? You might find yourself confronted with some imposing textbooks, the first few pages of which include indecipherable and impenetrable jargon, and be tempted to drop the class. Hopefully those books, like this one, will include glossaries that can provide an initial orientation to your endeavor. Otherwise, Google any terms you do not recognize. Wikipedia entries are sometimes reliable, although even first-year theology students should get in the habit of consulting scholarly sources that have been vetted by peer-review processes.

> *Read with understanding and don't be afraid to ask questions.*

Realize that most first-year theology classes, especially in Christian colleges and universities, are either required or serve to fulfill general requirements in the core curriculum. Christian institutions of higher education will usually feature theology courses that introduce students to the breadth of the tradition but yet also cultivate an appreciation for the specific church or movement with which the school may be affiliated. If one is there to pass the course and move on, then it is wise to pay attention to the syllabus and do what it says, on time. Success as desired usually follows in this case.

But if this book has been convincing at all, then hopefully you will take these courses with the expectation that they will equip you to live faithfully and creatively as a Christian who will confront circumstances that your textbooks can never adequately anticipate. For such, then, read with understanding and don't be afraid to ask questions. Your initial assignments will often invite reflection precisely along these lines: summarize what you have read, critically ask questions of what you understand, and try to apply such to your life, church, or ministry.

One hopes that your course will be structured in ways that provide you with ample opportunities to discuss the assigned readings. In traditional classrooms, perhaps there will be discussion groups. But more and more even in residential programs, there are online components that provide platforms for such theological conversation and interaction. Certainly, these will be *the* medium of engagement in fully online programs or classes. Do not overlook these as spaces for working out your ideas. Your classmates will inform and correct you, even as you can do the same for them. If there are particularly egregious misunderstandings in these online deliberations, the course instructor should be present and intervene. Or perhaps there will be a more informed teaching or graduate assistant who can ensure that perspective is provided.

Online posting and then writing assignments are occasions for you to demonstrate that you have read and understood enough of the material to turn around and think with or ask critical and constructive questions of what is being considered. If the instructor allows or invites, then bring other materials into your writing to show how you are connecting the dots. In online environments, the so-called flipped nature of instruction means that students are or need to be self-motivated learners who engage the assignments and bring them into conversation with their peers, with their prior or background learning, and be dialoguing with external sources, primarily but not necessarily only online. In these cases or circumstances, there are ample opportunities to research and review how the material under consideration is being received, deployed, or put to work in other contexts. These other voices and perspectives can be confusing for the novice, but that is part of the process for sorting out what one finds within a community of learners. We will gradually be shaped by the resulting and ongoing conversation. For these preliminary theological exercises, however, the goal is to attempt to digest the readings sufficiently so that one can discern their relevance to our lives.

> *Theological learning is a spiritual exercise.*

There is no reason why one's theological readings and assignments cannot be used as prompts for meditation and contemplation, where appropriate. Part of the point here is that theological learning is a spiritual exercise. This means not only that we invite the Holy Spirit—on a momentary, daily, or regular basis—to be present with us as we grapple with new questions, concepts, and ideas. It also means that we engage with these matters as an integral part of our ongoing spiritual practice. There is no need to divide what we do in or for the classroom from what we do in our prayer closets or in our liturgical spaces. Yes, we can't turn in our writing assignments and say only that we prayed about them but did not engage with the reading or attend to the specifics of what was required. But we ought to read, research, draft, dialogue, revise, and so forth in the Spirit. As it is written, "Whatever you do, in word or deed, do everything in the name of the Lord Jesus, giving thanks to God the Father through him" (Col. 3:17). This goes for everything we do in our theology classes no less than when we are in chapel.

7.2. The Theological Research Paper or Project

At some point, perhaps in this first theology course, or perhaps in a second-year class, or surely by the time of a final-year capstone seminar, you will need to write a theological research paper. Standard perhaps for lower levels is ten pages (double spaced) or about three thousand words (usually notes or bibliography are extra). The following steps are not sequentially sacrosanct, but a decent if not excellent final product will require attentiveness to each recommendation.

First, be sure to understand what the writing assignment or project asks for. The course syllabus should provide the pertinent parameters, and instructors or aides will not (or should not) turn away questions. Knowing what is due and by when should prompt you to anticipate what needs to be done and how much time you need to put aside for each step or element. If the paper requires a minimum number of research sources, be sure you plan in advance to search for such materials. A short paper could be written in one day (and it will also reflect that it was a rush job), but the research itself cannot be done by sitting down the day before the paper is due to finally begin working on it. Seasoned theological instructors will be able to recognize that you have not invested research effort into the assignment as designed to be a part of the learning process.

Second, theological research assignments are usually open enough to be pursued in any number of directions. If such latitude is intended, it never hurts to think in advance about how your own interests might be relatedly channeled. In such a case, it behooves you to confirm that this is acceptable with your instructor, particularly if there is any concern that your proposed topic is not quite related to the assignment. Either in person or via e-mail, suggest the topic and briefly indicate how you feel it pertains to what is expected. Redirection earlier in the term, if warranted, will save you time later.

Third, a research assignment involves research! Most college and university libraries have wonderful online databases that give students access to hundreds of thousands of full-text articles, and also an increasing number of books, at their preferred workstations. Read, take notes, and be sure to include the full bibliographic references (various electronic tools are now available to help you keep track of this information) with your notes as you go. Pay attention to the footnotes and bibliographies of what you are reading to follow the argument wherever your interests take you. Sometimes you might stop researching when you have reached whatever minimum number of sources you need to show. Those who are captivated by the theological exercise, however, will be inhibited only because time has run out. The paper is due at the end of the term or semester, sometimes long after you have read many more sources than required.

Fourth, at some point you will want to ensure that you have a coherent main idea, along with a related set of ideas, to constitute your paper. This involves clarifying your thoughts with a basic synopsis or abstract of your main theme, usually between 75 and 150 words, and an outline of how you are going to organize the primary and supporting points. It never hurts to run what you have drafted by your instructor if such questions are welcomed. This is all the more reason to get to work early on such things: this kind of feedback is impossible if you wait until the last minute.

> *Our prayer without ceasing means that even the process of deciding what to research and write can be spiritually discerned.*

Fifth, begin writing the paper. Ensure that you have a good introduction that includes the basic thesis and a map of the paper (usually highlighting how the sections of the paper contribute to the argument). The main parts of the paper should line up with how you have introduced them up front (or review and revise the introduction as needed). The conclusion then reiterates your main points and perhaps suggests what might need to be done next. Computerized writing makes it so much easier to revise what you have written and correct your text.

It is never too early, even if your theology paper is part of your first semester or term in college, to ensure that the style and format of your paper meets the expectations and preferences of your instructor, your major, and your institution as a whole. The discipline of theology, broadly speaking, usually falls back to the styles of either Turabian or Chicago. As a theologian who has had social science majors in classes or who works in interdisciplinary settings, I welcome APA, MLA, or other formats so long as students use each consistently and accurately. The course syllabus or instructor may specify preferences.

Finally, proofread your paper, attending to the coherence of argument and immaculateness of style. As an instructor and professor, I would rather engage your ideas than be distracted by formatting issues, typographical errors, grammatical awkwardness, or other infelicities. Always use spell- and grammar-checkers, and make an appointment with the writing center if you are an international student or someone who is working with English as a second language. In such cases, it is all the more important to plan in advance so that you can finish your first draft on time to consult the writing center and make final revisions, *before* the final paper is due.

If our minor theological assignments ought to be spiritually undertaken, so much more should this be the case with major projects. Each moment of the preceding process ought to be approached as part of one's spiritual journey. Our prayer without ceasing means that even the process of deciding what to research and write can be spiritually discerned.

7.3. Theological Integration and the Christian University

Not all readers of this book will be theology majors, but even those who are will inevitably press forward in their theological voyage in an interdisciplinary manner. In this section I will speak briefly to both types of students, beginning with our theological wannabes.

Over a four-year course of study, young theologians are merely initiated into the theological craft. They will be engaged in scriptural studies, historical excavations (of the church and its teachings), and philosophical expeditions, all as part of their theological formation. As such, even the study of theology, more narrowly delineated, is a multidisciplinary venture. Those who are really committed might take a semester or year of biblical Hebrew or Koine Greek, even as a few Christian colleges and universities might offer Latin (if not, you can always inquire with the faculty to find someone to lead you in directed language studies).

Perhaps more challenging on the interdisciplinary front, however, is when the theological questions we have pertain to matters typically researched and studied in other domains. Theology of religions, for instance, might involve religious studies, or theology of the environment might require environmental studies, or political theology might steer one into the political sciences, and so forth. If a theology major takes four years, then research in any of these inter- or multidisciplinary directions will mean at least that one must be doubly committed in order to engage the issues in a way that has some scholarly integrity. One has to recognize the limitations of one's efforts precisely because of the complexity of the task. The challenge in any case will be to attend to what the other discipline or domain has to say on its own terms about the topic of interest rather than rushing to impose a theological lens or perspective on that material. As theologians, of course, in the end we return to our theological arena and attempt to translate insights gained elsewhere in a way that honors rather than obfuscates that other set of voices. This is easier said than done in some cases, though. Some Christian contexts may continue to see certain

> *Christian believers are all theologians because life involves thinking about God and God's relationship to the world.*

disciplinary perspectives as fundamentally misguided (for instance, conservative Christian schools view the evolutionary sciences this way) rather than as reliable dialogue partners in the common search for truth. The way forward in such cases is never easy, although I have written this book in part to suggest ways to navigate these turns.

On the other side, most Christian colleges and universities have some kind of theological requirement in their general education core so that all graduates in any major will have at least one course exposing them to the faith tradition. This book shows that even if you do not intend to pursue a career in theology, Christian believers are all theologians insofar as life involves thinking about God and the divine relationship to and with the world. Christian schools that take the faith seriously, however, will also invite, if not require, that faculty who teach in nontheological disciplines and departments have a plan

> *Since all truth is God's truth, every field of study opens another window of understanding into the world that God has created.*

to introduce and support students in a course of inquiry that integrates their major and its disciplines with fundamental elements of the faith. Majors often have capstone seminars in which the final project will include a section or component where such integration is demonstrated. In other words, beyond the personal and ecclesial benefits of studying theology (see the preceding two chapters), other majors than theology will also have occasion, in Christian contexts, to consider their program of study in some kind of theological light.

Here, the temptation may be the reverse: to impose their own disciplinary perspective, as the one they know better if not best, on their engagements with theology. The result here would be distortions not just for their theological understanding but also of the major areas of study. Qualified Christian teachers in these other disciplines are the best guides. They have (one hopes) spent some time thinking about their vocation, craft, and work from a faith-informed perspective and can guide novice students. The result will be a sturdier foundation for lifelong learning: the capacity to relate to theological resources all that we encounter on our often-meandering paths and the ability to query, from a theological point of view, what we keep learning. From this perspective, those not majoring in theology at Christian colleges and universities get to develop interdisciplinary skills for lifelong learning. This is an added benefit that their colleagues in secular tertiary educational systems miss out on.

The Day of Pentecost's promise that salvation arrives in and through the many tongues of human cultures may also be relevant in this regard. The many disciplines are also human cultural artifacts and constructs, each involving a certain set of practices (of inquiry) and requiring initiation (years of study). Since all truth is God's truth, so every disciplinary arena makes available another window of understanding into the world that God has created. This does not mean that everything discovered or claimed within established scientific and scholarly disciplines is truthful. But the process of peer review functions analogously to a prophetic community or to how the manifestation of charismatic gifts like prophecy ought to work in a congregation. "Let two or three prophets speak, and let the others weigh what is said" (1 Cor. 14:29). The latter process does not guarantee that the community will mis-hear the voice of the Spirit but provides a course of checks and balances designed to ward off the most egregious errors. So also, then, disciplinary discussion/ debate and peer review work by trial and error in search of the truth. Those not majoring in theology therefore can also call on the Holy Spirit for their journey. If they do, then they embark and stay on a rich life of learning involving conversation partners and perspectives that are not ecclesially delimited.

7.4. Theologizing as a Spiritual Discipline

Christian tertiary education will have a range of extracurricular activities like chapels, vespers, and Bible studies designed to support and enrich the faith component. Without minimizing the import of these venues for overall educational formation and development, my goal in this chapter has been to help students see in theological light what they do in their theology classes and other programs of study. This point has been repeated already: the Christian life of the mind is or ought to be inseparable from life in the Spirit. Hence it is not that we go to chapel to nurture our spiritual needs and to the classroom to feed our intellectual hunger. Instead, the educational path and its many activities ought to be engaged not just intellectually but also spiritually. Similarly, the spiritual life is theologically informed and thus for all majors also an interdisciplinary undertaking.

At this juncture, it is important to look backward in order to bring this chapter to a close. Recall that the two parts of this book have to do with the resources of theology and its practical purposes (or its purposive practices). Four chapters (1–4) above looked at theology derived from Scripture, tradition, reason, and experience, each as informing the other, albeit with Scripture as the primary authoritative source (even if not approachable except through the others). But our doing of theology is historically situated and contextually motivated. So the last three chapters have explored the practices of theology for our personal, ecclesial, and educational lives. In each segment, then, our theological reflection and consideration are scripturally, traditionally, rationally, and experientially forged. Sometimes the deliverances of the tradition prompt questions that lead us back to Scripture. At other times experiential dynamics lead us to revisit traditionally assumed positions and practices. In one moment or situation, reasoned argumentation is important, but in another setting practical relevance or experiential possibility is prioritized. But in all cases, each of the elements of the quadrilateral are in play, even if one might at any moment be more or less in the foreground or in the background.

This is why in our theological studies, even in this first year, the goals are multiple: (1) increasing familiarization with the biblical texts and the scholarly tools needed to further engage with them; (2) knowledge of the theological traditions; (3) reasoned dialogue, discussion, and debate with instructors and peers in our schools and with our family and friends from our homes and churches; and (4) exposure to as wide a range of experiences as possible and to persons who come from other backgrounds and can provide other perspectives to complement and challenge our own. Tertiary educational learning is all about grappling with new learning. The New Testament presents these as occasions for argument, reasoning together, debate, and dialogue (*dialogos*, the base word in Acts 17:2, 17; 18:4; 19:8–9), so

> *Be alert to the breath of God and come to see activities in your studies as answers to your prayers.*

that we grapple with the many viewpoints in our struggle to discover the truth. All of this activity, we suggest, is part of our spiritual journey and ought to be undertaken while continuously invoking the Holy Spirit and depending on divine grace.

Our readings, reflections, and conversations can and should be prompts for reflection. These can be concretely included in our daily rhythms by notetaking or journaling. We might take notes in relationship to our ongoing reading and research, or journal in our devotional practice. These are two sides to one coin, each allowing for us to reflect on why what we are recording is important to us. If we want to invite further interaction on these thoughts, we might consider a blog or mode of social media that might allow us to share what we are discovering and invite responses. Handwritten notes or journaling might be the most intimate. Yet they are also more difficult to absorb into our formal writing since we cannot deploy the "search," "find," "copy," and "paste" functions of word processors and weave these ideas later into our assignments or papers.

In any case, even if in a more solitary manner (of journaling or note-taking) or more public domain (e.g., in a blog or via social media), such written reflections are occasions of dialogue, with our self and with others. Dialogue is a form of experiential reasoning, one consistent with the Day of Pentecost miracle of many tongues coming together, through which the glory of God appears and is manifest (even if amid confusion and cacophony). In such dialogical activities, then, Scripture is constantly consulted, and tradition is renewed and reformed in the process. Our journaling, note-taking, assignment writing, paper production, and project completion cumulatively will reveal, over time, our development as young theologians.

Do not therefore despise these early days and weeks in your first theology course or in your program of study. They are part of this chapter of your life, one that builds on all of the preceding developments and opens up new vistas and opportunities for next steps. You know in faith that the same Holy Spirit who has led you to this new educational environment will carry you through its demands and requirements, even if the presence and activity of the divine Spirit remains by and large imperceptible. But attempt to be alert to the breath of God, cultivate the blowing of that wind, and come to see activities in your studies as answers to your prayers.

Discussion Questions

1. Write down how you practice the presence of the Holy Spirit in your daily rhythms. Ask someone else to share with you their own experiences, expectations, and practices in this regard.

2. Think back to the last successful paper you wrote (maybe in high school). What did you do there that made it a pleasant and enjoyable experience and that you might be able to add to the steps discussed in §7.2 above?

3. If you are not a theology major, find one, and vice versa; discuss with each other why your work might gain from the perspective of your discussion partner. What are the possibilities and pitfalls of such interaction between these different areas of study?

4. Have Scripture, tradition, reason, and experience shaped you theologically so far? How else might the Holy Spirit continue to use these sources to form you spiritually and educationally?

For Further Reading

Alexander, Irene. *A Glimpse of the Kingdom in Academia: Academic Formation as Radical Discipleship*. Eugene, OR: Cascade Books, 2013.

Cepero, Helen. *Journaling as a Spiritual Practice: Encountering God through Attentive Writing*. Downers Grove, IL: IVP Books, 2008.

Jacobsen, Rhonda Hustedt, and Douglas Jacobsen. *Scholarship and Christian Faith: Enlarging the Conversation*. Oxford: Oxford University Press, 2004.

Lonergan, Bernard J. F. *Method in Theology*. New York: Herder & Herder, 1972.

Noll, Mark A. *The Scandal of the Evangelical Mind*. Grand Rapids: Wm. B. Eerdmans Publishing Co., 1995.

Palmer, Parker J. *To Know as We Are Known: Education as a Spiritual Journey*. San Francisco: HarperOne, 1993.

Ream, Todd C., Timothy W. Herrmann, and C. Skip Trudeau. *A Parent's Guide to the Christian College: Supporting Your Child's Mind and Spirit during the College Years*. Abilene, TX: Abilene Christian University Press, 2011.

Ryken, Leland. *The Christian Imagination: Essays on Literature and the Arts*. Grand Rapids: Baker Book House, 1981.

Smith, James K. A. *Desiring the Kingdom: Worship, Worldview, and Cultural Formation*. Grand Rapids: Baker Academic, 2009.

Timmerman, John H., and Donald R. Hettinga. *In the World: Reading and Writing as a Christian*. Grand Rapids: Baker Academic, 2004.

Vyhmeister, Nancy Jean. *Quality Research Papers: For Students of Religion and Theology*. 2nd ed. Grand Rapids: Zondervan, 2008.

Wolterstorff, Nicholas P. *Educating for Life: Reflections on Christian Teaching and Learning*. Edited by Gloria Goris Stronks and Clarence W. Joldersma. Grand Rapids: Baker Academic, 2002.

Yong, Amos, and Dale M. Coulter. *Finding the Holy Spirit at a Christian University: Renewing Christian Higher Education*. Grand Rapids: Wm. B. Eerdmans Publishing Co., forthcoming in 2019.

8

Theology as Charismatic Practice

Theology by the Spirit, Trinitarian Theologians

This final chapter of part II steps back to consider the bigger developmental and theological picture behind the practices in our personal, ecclesial, and educational lives. In our discussion about these three venues of theological practice, we have been constantly alerted to the role of the Holy Spirit in facilitating our theological efforts: to grow us spiritually, to enable the church's mission collectively, and to form us educationally. Here we turn our attention to a theology of the Spirit in order to better appreciate the pneumatological thread that has been woven through both parts of this book. This is also important since the Spirit works to save and transform fallen human creatures, not to call attention to the Spirit! So, in these last few pages, we consider pneumatology to gain perspective.

I begin with a more autobiographical approach here because of the experiential dimension and source of all theologizing that we have already discussed more abstractly. I proceed to discuss, in sequence, being a pneumatological theologian and being a Trinitarian theologian. The concluding section summarizes how we can see our personal, ecclesial, and educational lives and practices in pneumatological and Trinitarian terms.

I hope that my readers will reflect on their own theological sojourns so far, however brief, as they consider my experiences. I invite you to consider specifically that Christian theologians, however young and aspiring, all do theology not just after Easter but also after Pentecost. Yet our paths of inquiry lead, or ought to open us up, to an ever more fully and intentionally Trinitarian theology. In my humble opinion, those who grasp this important theological point will have taken another big step along their way to becoming true theologians.

8.1. Starting with the Spirit

My parents have been ministers in the Assemblies of God (AG) Church, a pentecostal denomination, from even before I was born (and still are pastorally active as of the time of writing of this book!). When I was ten years old, our family moved from the country of Malaysia, where I and my two younger siblings were born, to northern California, where my parents took up pastoral ministry at a small mission church dedicated to serving Chinese-speaking and bilingual immigrants and their families. I went from being a cross-cultural pastor's kid (PK) to being a transcontinental missionary kid (MK) overnight. During my teen years, I attended church as regularly as I could (sometimes staying home to watch my younger brother who was born with Down syndrome). I also was very involved in our summer church-camp-based Bible-quiz program for the dozen churches or so in our Chinese-speaking group of churches (at one point having committed to memory the entire New Testament).

When I was in middle school I had profound experiences of the Holy Spirit in our summer camp sessions. This included speaking in tongues, which our church and denomination understood as signifying the baptism of the Spirit that empowered our witness and testimony. When I became a junior in high school, I helped my parents by starting our first official youth group in the church. During my senior year, I felt a call to ministry. I went off to Bethany Bible College, an AG-affiliated school (which unfortunately closed in 2009).

> When I became a theologian, I could not be anything other than a pentecostal theologian.

If there was any doubt about my pentecostal identity while growing up as a pentecostal PK and MK, my four-year undergraduate experience sealed the deal. I met my wife at Bethany, to whom I am still married thirty-plus years, three children, and one granddaughter later. She also was raised, since her teen years, in a church in Eastern Washington that was part of the Latin American Spanish district of the AG. I was credentialed as an AG minister during my final year at Bethany. We then landed a youth pastorate at an AG church in the Bay Area. In large part because we were unprepared for the challenges of our cross-cultural marriage, our pastoral work lasted only one year. We had to take "time out" in order to cherish our young and (then) fragile marriage.

I enrolled in Western Evangelical Seminary (WES), Portland, Oregon (now Portland Seminary), for two reasons. First, tuition reimbursement was available to me through my employer (the state of Washington's Department of Social and Health Services at that point). Second, going to seminary was at that time the only way I knew how to attempt to redeem the "failure" of our youth pastorate. If before WES I presumed that all true Christians were pentecostal of the sort I was, I was quickly disabused of this idea. My exposure to those from other churches whose Christian identities were undeniable led me to wonder if my pentecostal convictions were necessary, much less defensible. During the first year or two of my seminary studies, I almost left my AG church. But I had a couple of phone conversations with one of my Bethany professors who was completing his PhD in theology at a so-called liberal theological school. He gave me permission to not make such decisions too quickly. It was OK to proceed slowly even if I did not have all the answers to my questions.

It was over my four-plus years at WES that it first dawned on me that I could be a theologian, and a pentecostal theologian at that. I learned and wrote about pentecostal history in my Christian history class. In my Christian thought class I also discovered how theological ideas developed, even pentecostal theologies. The year after I graduated from WES (1993), I went to my first meeting of the Society for Pentecostal Studies. One of my WES professors (not a pentecostal) encouraged me to get involved. There I met pentecostal scholars, an oxymoron then indeed! They showed me that it was possible to remain a Spirit-filled believer and yet think critically and participate in the intellectual life.

Readers of this book might now be able to better understand why the role of the Spirit is so prominent in this book. Growing up pentecostal, the work of the Spirit was presumed in all we did as believers. Hence, when I became a theologian, I could not be anything other than a pentecostal theologian. This was my path. Others who have grown up pentecostal have taken other routes. My point is not a deterministic position that our past delimits our future. Instead, in hindsight, we might be able to appreciate how our present identity and vocation have roots deep in our past experiences.

Why are you at this college (rather than another), in this program (instead of another), and in this class (did you have an elective option)? How have your life circumstances opened up some possibilities, and how have your decisions at those moments shaped you in some ways but foreclosed other developments as well? How are the choices you might make today, in this class, course of study, college, or university, going to influence what happens next?

8.2. Theologizing after Easter and after Pentecost

Not surprisingly, then, when I enrolled in a doctoral program of theological study, I pursued a very pentecostal question: how might I develop a pentecostal perspective on living in a world of many religions? Questions germinating during my seminary experience formed the backdrop to this: how could I square my prior conviction that all true Christians were pentecostal with my growing realization that many if not most Christians were not pentecostal? The horizons of this question were extended during my second master's program of study in intellectual history and the history of philosophy (at Portland State University): how could I reconcile my belief that only Christians were saved with the growing realization that many if not most people around the world, and historically, were not Christian but members, devotees, or adherents of other faith traditions? My doctoral thesis sought to develop a pneumatological approach to this last question in relationship to the Day of Pentecost narrative (Acts 2) central to pentecostal spirituality. It was published later as *Discerning the Spirit(s): A Pentecostal-Charismatic Contribution to Christian Theology of Religions* (in Sheffield Academic Press's Journal of Pentecostal Theology Supplement Series in 2000).

Almost all of my work in the last twenty years (almost fifty authored and edited books plus hundreds of journal articles and book chapters) has taken off from this set of pentecostal and pneumatological questions opened up by my doctoral research. But since the initial impulses were aligned by my growing up pentecostal and being a minister in a pentecostal church (the AG), this has gradually led to the conviction, and accompanying arguments, that all Christian experience is pentecostal in some respect and therefore all Christian theology has a pentecostal character. Three interrelated reasons drive this work: biblical, traditional, and experiential.

First, biblically, Christian faith is assuredly based on Jesus Christ, who was the Messiah, the one anointed by the divine Spirit. In that sense, Christian theology is after the incarnation, including the life, death, resurrection, and ascension of Jesus as the man of the Spirit. Thus Christian theologizing proceeds after Easter, so that even the documents of the New Testament themselves are from the perspective and experience of the Christ raised from the dead by the power of the Holy Spirit (see Rom. 1:4). Yet according to the writings of the same Christian canon, the apostolic experience was based not only on Jesus' resurrection but also inspired by his pouring out of the Holy Spirit on the Day of Pentecost. Hence, Christian writing, experience, and thinking are both post-Easter and post-Pentecost. As such, why would not all Christian theologizing since also be post-Easter and post-Pentecost? I urge that it is but that we have not often thought about our efforts in this way.

> *Christian experience is pneumatological: we come into Christian faith and life only through the Holy Spirit.*

Yet surely the Orthodox, Roman Catholic, and Protestant traditions are mostly Trinitarian in recognizing and confessing the Holy Spirit as the third divine person alongside the Father and the Son. I say *mostly* because there are a few very marginal movements that are either anti-Trinitarian or non-Trinitarian, for various historic reasons. But even then, to the degree that they are biblical, they recognize that Christian theology has to do with the Father, Son, and Holy Spirit. Hence there is a real sense in which Christianity is Trinitarian, as is Christian theology, even if pneumatology, or the study of the person and work of the Spirit, has been underplayed more often than not historically. Yet the resurgence of pneumatology and of Trinitarian theology has grown hand in hand over the last fifty years. Pentecostal theologians like myself have been blessed to have played a role in some of these developments.

Last but not least, Christian experience is pneumatological. We come into Christian faith and life only through the Holy Spirit. "He saved us," Paul writes, "not because of any works of righteousness that we had done, but according to his mercy, through the water of rebirth and renewal by the Holy Spirit" (Titus 3:5). Luke records Peter's answer to the most fundamental question of all: "What should we do?" Peter declares, "Repent, and be baptized every one of you in the name of Jesus Christ so that your sins may be forgiven; and you will receive the gift of the Holy Spirit" (Acts 2:37–38). In short, again, even if we might not operate consciously from this truth, the reality is that our Christian lives are from the beginning pentecostal and pneumatological, made possible by the work of the Holy Spirit.

You, my patient readers, may not have thought much about this yourself, even if you were raised or have been formed in pentecostal churches. Yet whatever our Christian background, consider that we become members of the body of Christ through the Holy Spirit (1 Cor. 12:12–13). Our churches all confess the reality of the Spirit, however that is understood, and affirm that Christian life and discipleship are possible because Jesus, from the right hand of the Father, has poured out the Spirit upon all flesh (Acts 2:33). So, from that perspective, each of us are Christians by the Spirit and have embarked on this next chapter of our lives as aspiring young theologians precisely in the Spirit. We are pentecostal and pneumatological theologians in fact and in actuality, even if not in name, and that is the way it should be as the Spirit guides us.

8.3. Pentecostal Perspective, Trinitarian Theologian

Yet since the Spirit focuses us on God in Christ, not on the Spirit, the Spirit provides perspective for theology as a whole, not just for pneumatology (theology of the Spirit). In that respect, all pentecostal theology is pneumatological, by and through the Spirit; but to what ends? To christological and, more specifically, Trinitarian ends. In the Fourth Gospel, Jesus says that the Spirit "will teach you everything, and remind you of all that I have said to you" (John 14:26b), and "will testify on my behalf" (15:26b). Further, John says, "he will not speak on his own, but will speak whatever he hears, and he will declare to you the things that are to come. He will glorify me, because he will take what is mine and declare it to you" (16:13b–14). This means that the Spirit's work ultimately lifts up Jesus. This is the eschatological goal of the Spirit's revealing message. Perhaps the Son is only implicit in the Spirit's achievements on this side of the eschaton. Yet viewed from the perspective of the end, "When all things are subjected to him, then the Son himself will also be subjected to the one who put all things in subjection under him, so that God may be all in all" (1 Cor. 15:28).

> *Theology orients us toward the truth of the one God who has revealed himself in Christ by the Spirit.*

The Nicene Creed leads us to confess: "We believe in one God . . . , in one Lord Jesus Christ . . . , and in the Holy Spirit. . . ." Modern Christians are also singing the words of the hymn "Holy, Holy, Holy," written by Reginald Heber (1783–1826): "God in three persons, blessed Trinity." As those created in the image of God, we experience these scripturally unveiled mysteries as personal. This is so even if explicating the reality of the one God as "not three Gods," as in the famously titled apologetic treatise of the Cappadocian theologian Gregory of Nyssa, has never been easy. Christian monotheism means that we affirm personally by the Spirit that God is one, albeit revealed as Father, Son, and Spirit.

My hopes for this book include accomplishing two things. First, to alert us to our identity as pentecostal theologians who attempt to think God's thoughts after the Day of Pentecost's outpouring of the Holy Spirit by Jesus. Second, to orient us toward the truth of the one God who has revealed himself in Christ by the Spirit. These are less logical conundrums to be resolved than a spiritual path to be traversed. Paul taught that "hope does not disappoint us, because God's love has been poured into our hearts through the Holy Spirit that has been given to us" (Rom. 5:5). Building on this text, Augustine of Hippo (354–430), one of the great theologians of the church, identified the Spirit as the love between the Father and the Son. He did this not in order to depersonalize the Spirit but to experience and enable inhabitation of this loving divine reality. From this perspective, life in the Spirit is an invitation to participate in and means of accessing the love of the triune God. In other words, we are enabled to love God precisely because God meets us by the Spirit as the divine love.

It is this overflowing love of God that is at the heart of all reality. In fact, the world in its beautiful complexity might be said also to be an expression of God the Lover. As such, we have a glimpse of this love also in our experience of love in this world: love of parents for children, love of siblings, love of friends for each other. Theological reflection provides us with moments to comprehend and articulate this love that we feel and by which we are sustained. Theological formulation attempts to name the mystery of Trinitarian love that we feel. This is not to claim that there is no ambiguity and pain in this life. It is to affirm that even amid conflicting experiences, the ineffable triune love shines through, drawing us forward in hope. Theological speech thereby sounds forth by the Spirit "with sighs too deep for words" (Rom. 8:26b). These are gestures that are refined in life but never fully captured in words.

You have found yourself in college, now studying theology, even as a neophyte—why? Some of you might want an undergraduate degree to get a good job and earn an honest living. Others of you might be here because your parents want you to be, or you are unsure what else to do, and this is what was expected or seemed like the next step in life after high school. Thus you can take this reading assignment or this class as simply checking off another item on your to-do list in order to graduate someday and move on to something else. Or you can see this as an invitation to embark on a lifelong passage of knowing the triune God by the divine Spirit. Through this knowledge, we can better understand ourselves and our place in the world God has created.

8.4. The Spirit Has the First, Initiating Word

Hence in this book and by the Spirit, we have come to see better the sources and practices of theology, in order to more clearly understand and participate in God's saving work in Christ. If the Spirit is the love of the Trinitarian reality of God and the mediating power, in Christ, of that redemptive mystery, then it makes sense that the Spirit is also the gift of life that moves us on the track toward that destination. In this book, our focus has been on doing theology on the beginning portion of that trail. It is now time to make some transitional comments in closing. We know that we start with the Spirit, but if Christian faith is right that life in Christ is eternal life with God, then there is no last word. Every succeeding word is a prelude to another word, not to wear us out but to strengthen us for what is next.

> *As long as the wind of God blows through our bodies, there will always be a next moment to ponder, to deliberate, and to theologize.*

So, by now we know that in many respects, theology is complicated. There are four sources that we discussed, and each of them is not easily dissected and understood. It would have been easier to just have the Bible tell us clearly about God, Christ, and salvation, right? Or could not the church's creeds and confessions have put these truths in plain language? Or could we not have been created to easily think through and summarize in a few words what or who God is? Yet, on the other hand, we as human creatures get to theologize. We get to wonder about these things and ask more and more complex questions along the way. At the time of writing this book, I have a granddaughter who comes on FaceTime with my wife and asks, "Where's Grandpa?" This makes my heart leap with joy. She will continue to ask many other questions in life. Maybe she will become a more profound theologian than the grandfather she occasionally now wonders about.

Theologizing is a verb specifying what we do as human creatures, enabled by the divine breath that animates our lungs, in our efforts to love God, others, and life with all we are, including our minds and intellects. Thus our first theology class, perhaps early in our program of study, provides us with an opportunity to practice our first, however faltering, movements of theologizing. These first reflection assignments, or the final paper for this term or quarter, represent our baby steps in learning how to theologize. These will enlarge toward toddler and childish scurrying wherein our devotional lives are complicated as we shift from a faith-filled approach to our Bible reading/memorization to a faith-seeking-understanding stance. We will develop into taking adult strides as we bring our enhanced perspectives to our churches and contribute to the apostolic mission of bearing witness to the God of Jesus Christ in the world. As long as the wind of God blows through our bodies, there will always be a next moment to ponder, to deliberate, and to theologize. That is our call and gift as theologians, which may be frustrating at times but also is part of what gives life meaning and satisfaction. We may not always arrive at definitive answers (even if along the way, some resolutions emerge). But we will have another opportunity to refine our questions. Even in eternity, we experience rest but also the activity of worshiping God and eternally fathoming yet deeper the love that holds us. (If God is infinite, then finite, even if resurrected, human minds will with everlasting time still never come to fully grasp the divine, otherwise the creature would become creator.)

As young theologians, then, you are invited to open the pages of your Bible again and again. From there you will gain perspective even as you will be drawn into the triune mystery. Through this course you are also given permission to explore the depths of the theological traditions that you have now begun to name and identify. You will enlarge your pool of theological resources even as you will see dead ends and wrong turns that are just as instructive. You now know that asking hard questions is not only normal but also perhaps contrary to what you were led to believe and expected to do while growing up in your church. It is just that our questioning ought never to be on our own, but with others on life's path, whose twists and turns are never quite predictable, while always looking back to Scripture.

So, what if we go too far and wander from the confines of our Christian community and lose faith, or become something else, like a Muslim or whatever? Life is a risk, isn't it? Meeting the person who, we think, is our soul mate and getting married is equally a chance we take, even if our hearts flutter all the way through courtship to our wedding date. But if we could control our marriages, our spouses would be miserable and we would be less than human. Similarly, our walk with God, in Christ and by the Spirit, requires courage. For "without faith it is impossible to please God, for whoever would approach him must believe that he exists and that he rewards those who seek him" (Heb. 11:6). Love God, trust the Spirit, walk with others in the body of Christ, be hospitable to strangers, embrace others who are on the road, and don't forget to keep asking for directions.

Discussion Questions

1. What are the ecclesial traditions that have shaped your life so far? What emphasis, if any, has there been on the person and work of the Holy Spirit in your churches so far?
2. "All Christians are Pentecostals; they just don't know it!" How would you respond to this comment at this time?
3. "I am a pentecostal, pneumatological, and Trinitarian theologian!" Argue about this autobiographically with yourself and theologically with someone else.
4. Identify the role of the Holy Spirit in your personal/devotional life, in your church participation, in your studies, and in your life in the world. How can you be more intentional about a Spirit-filled life in each of these areas?

For Further Reading

Bingemer, Maria Clara Lucchetti. *A Face for God: Reflections on Trinitarian Theology for Our Times*. Miami: Convivium Press, 2014.

Chandler, Diane J. *Christian Spiritual Formation: An Integrated Approach for Personal and Relational Wholeness*. Downers Grove, IL: IVP Academic, 2014.

Downey, Michael. *Altogether Gift: A Trinitarian Spirituality*. Maryknoll, NY: Orbis Books, 2000.

Fettke, Steven M., and Robby Waddell, eds. *Pentecostals in the Academy: Testimonies of Call*. Cleveland, TN: CPT Press, 2012.

Marshall, Molly T. *Joining the Dance: A Theology of the Spirit*. Valley Forge, PA: Judson Press, 2003.

McClendon, James William, Jr. *Biography as Theology: How Life Stories Can Remake Today's Theology*. Nashville: Abingdon Press, 1974.

Nañez, Rick. *Full Gospel, Fractured Minds? A Call to Use God's Gift of the Intellect*. Grand Rapids: Zondervan, 2005.

Noll, Mark A. *Jesus Christ and the Life of the Mind*. Grand Rapids: Wm. B. Eerdmans Publishing Co., 2013.

Pinnock, Clark H. *Flame of Love: A Theology of the Holy Spirit*. Downers Grove, IL: InterVarsity Press, 1996.

Preece, Gordon, and Stephen Pickard, eds. *Starting with the Spirit*. Hindmarsh: Australian Theological Forum, 2001.

Tomlin, Graham. *The Prodigal Spirit: The Trinity, the Church, and the Future of the World*. London: Alpha International, 2011.

Yong, Amos. *Spirit of Love: A Trinitarian Theology of Grace*. Waco, TX: Baylor University Press, 2012.

Appendix

Becoming a Professional Theologian

Getting There from Here

The following provides concrete guidelines for (1) how to discern if one is called to be a professional theologian, (2) how to engage the theological academy and its various and associated guilds, and (3) how to navigate graduate-level theological education, all as part and parcel of (4) cultivating the intellectual life as central to life in the Spirit. If your first theology class incites your imagination, keep in mind these suggestions in order to anticipate some possible next steps in the next few years. But along the way, do not forget to enjoy the rest of your undergraduate (or graduate) experience, especially other theology classes that you might have the opportunity to take.

Discerning the Call to Graduate/Doctoral Theological Education

How does one move from undergraduate to graduate theological study? First and foremost, one intuits that one has the aptitude and passion for pursuing the issues we have already covered in this book. Does study excite you, and can you not wait to get out of bed in order to go back to your computer or to visit the library? Are you becoming convinced that the theological course is less to solve the puzzles of the universe and more about deepening your perspective in order to love and serve God and others better?

Then one's family and friends, and especially pastors and college instructors and mentors, will be helpful in sparking or confirming one's vocational interests. Some of our pastors might not be in the best position to encourage our theological curiosities. But those who have benefited from a seminary or theological education, perhaps increasingly obvious to you now that you've had your own initial exposure to these matters, would be good discussion partners as you discern your way forward. Your theology professors in particular, especially those who take seriously their own mentoring responsibilities, will also invite you to consider next steps, first by taking other theology electives or by honing your theological skills in other courses you might take. You might get an e-mail even after the semester is over, once your professor has had a chance to read your final paper, saying something like this: "Great job! Come talk to me more if you think you might want to study theology further!" That is a wonderful sign and cue from someone who has run through the graduate-program mill and recognizes that you have the potential to excel in this venture.

The sooner you recognize that you have a theological appetite, the sooner you can devote yourself to being a theology major or integrating theological interests into the rest of your undergraduate studies. As already indicated, Christian college and university instructors and professors in any major or class will be interested in you and should be able to assist your own youthful theological efforts to think through issues in whatever classes or courses you take. Each class, semester, and year will add layers of perspective and expertise to your tool kit.

There are many postgraduate theological programs you might consider. For those interested in pursuing ministerial-related vocations, seminaries provide master's-level theological instruction as stand-alone institutions, often but not always affiliated with churches. Yet seminaries also are effective in preparing one for doctoral studies in theology. Divinity schools, in some institutions known as theological schools, do similar things but are embedded within university systems. They have the benefit of extending the interdisciplinary studies that you might have received in a liberal arts college or Christian university undergraduate context. You could also opt to pursue graduate theological study in departments of religion at a range of religiously and nonreligiously affiliated universities. Consult with your college professors and mentors in theology. They can help to identify options suitable to your temperament, aspirations, capabilities or gifts, and contextual circumstances.

If you are convinced that you want to teach religion or theology at least at the undergraduate level, you will need a doctorate in theology. Today there are a few doctor of theology (ThD) programs in some university divinity or theological schools. But the more prominent degree is the doctor of philosophy (PhD) in theology or affiliated areas. A very small handful of the latter invite students straight from their undergraduate programs onto the doctoral path, during which one earns a master's degree. Most PhDs, however, involve completion of one or more master's-level degrees (I have two myself). This includes the master of theology (ThM), an intermediate step between the master's and doctoral programs of study.

There are other professionally oriented doctoral programs that are more usually focused on developing leadership skills and certifying competence in the field. The doctor of ministry (DMin) or doctor of missiology (DMiss) are offered mostly in seminary contexts, and obtaining such degrees often qualifies one to teach in programs devoted to ministerial or missiological training. Whereas these degrees support and elevate the standing of ministry and mission practitioners, the ThD and PhD routes of study are designed to propel the research, writing, scholarship, and teaching that sustain professorial vocations. The reality in many places today, however, is that many PhD degree holders are unable to find teaching or related positions in academia, especially in the United States, because of the shrinking job market (universities eliminating religion programs or seminaries downsizing, consistent with shrinking attendance in many mainline Protestant churches and denominations). Yet opportunities exist abroad.

If figuring out what to write for one's first theology paper is a spiritual activity, so is deciding if and where to go next to further one's postgraduate theological education. Hearing the Spirit's voice in regard to the latter possibilities, however, involves identifying how such a course of study will be funded. Graduate-level studies, in theology no less, are expensive and unaffordable for most people, so if this is of God, provision will be there. There are scholarships available from churches or a variety of organizations that you ought to look for early in the process of discernment. The academic scholarship, however, is usually based on merit, usually related to indicators of potential for academic achievement. Remember: the charismatic activities of the Spirit are not necessarily disconnected from hard academic work!

Welcome to the Guild/s

So how does one produce a record not necessarily of accomplishment but also of potential in the field? How might your application to graduate programs, master's first and then doctoral levels, capture the attention of admissions officers and faculty members to funnel whatever (often meager) scholarship or financial resources to you rather than someone else? One's résumé coming out of college (or out of one's master's degree later) should lift up signs of your engagement with the field of theology in its various spheres precisely in order to show that you are already committed to this line of inquiry and have advanced beyond baby steps in this direction. The more of the following is evident in your application, the stronger a candidate you will be, not just for admission but also for the most prestigious—and lucrative!—scholarships that might be available.

First, in conversation with your theology professor and mentors, identify the handful of scholarly societies in which you ought to take out student membership in order to keep abreast of developments in the guild. Graduate-level education, including in theological studies, is supported by various academic societies. Student membership costs something, but this is a good investment. You thus will get the society's scholarly journals (often multiple issues in any year), in and through which you read about new books in the field, become further familiarized with areas of debate, follow the developing conversation, and begin to recognize the experts who are writing articles or being quoted or cited in these pieces. Regularly reading these journals will stir further interest, direct your reading and imagination, and expand your base of knowledge (which range will begin to impress your readers).

Your student membership, however, will also bring alerts to the annual nationally and even internationally organized meetings that most scholarly societies hold. Some of the larger ones, like the American Academy of Religion, the Society of Biblical Literature, or the Evangelical Theological Society, have a second set of regional meetings you can attend. Take time out to sign up for one of these meetings as soon as possible. These will allow you to experience live and in the flesh what you read about in the journals: presentations of papers by faculty experts and neophyte graduate students, hallway discussions of the latest debates and issues, book exhibits to peruse the newest publications, and so forth. These meetings provide opportunities for networking with others who have similar theological interests. You will meet authors of books you have read and perhaps make acquaintance with a future teacher/mentor, editor, or publisher.

After you have been to one of these meetings in person, then watch for announcements regarding the next national or regional meeting and the attending call for papers. These calls invite you to submit a proposal to present a paper or discuss an idea at the meeting. Your proposal is vetted by experts (the gatekeepers organizing these conferences). If you are invited to make your presentation, your name appears on the program. So, for your second conference, you get to talk about your ideas while others listen and respond. Of course, ask your mentor to review your proposal before submission to ensure that it is as strong as possible. Getting your proposal accepted allows you to list such on your résumé or budding curriculum vitae (the academic and longer version of résumés).

From presentation at a conference, you might next consider sending your paper to a journal to be considered for publication. Hopefully the paper you present will already have been reviewed by your professor or mentor, perhaps as part of some research and writing you did in a prior course, after which you were encouraged to develop the paper. And if the reception of your ideas at the conference was positive and encouraging, even if not uncritical, revise it further and then identify a possible scholarly journal in which it might fit. You might not get published initially, but going through the process itself is helpful. The truth is that all academics have experienced rejection of their papers, essays, or articles at some point. But if and when you get a first acceptance for publication, this might be followed by a second.

Backtracking for a moment, your first publication might instead be a book review. Don't forget to carefully consider the book review sections of each new issue of the journals you receive. This not only enables you to follow the ongoing discussion but also provides some orientation to writing your own review. In any case you will want to read new books in the field. So why not e-mail the book review editor of these journals, whose name and contact information is usually inside the front or back cover of the journal, or else available from the journal's home Web page? Tell them what program of study you are in and offer to write a review of a new book for that journal. Master's-level students are perhaps in the best situation to initiate offers that will be accepted in this way. A book review takes much less effort, involves engaging a text that one might be reading anyway for any set of reasons, and provides practice for sharpening your writing and analytical skills.

Any and all of these activities—membership in a scholarly society, presenting a paper at a conference, getting published whether as a book reviewer or essay author—goes onto your résumé or vitae. The more line items as such on your application, the more commendable you are not just for acceptance into graduate programs but also for the scholarship and funds set aside for the most promising students. Maybe the Spirit will provide for at least part of your graduate education in this way. Certainly the process of getting this far itself will significantly shape your life's pilgrimage.

Navigating Graduate School

Once accepted into graduate school, you will of course need to believe that God will provide the funding needed so that you do not go into (excessive) debt even as you work hard. Beyond this economic or financial aspect, however, here are some tips toward success at that level. I mention these here in part because the following provides an occasion to remind us that there are some basic principles to academic success whether one is just starting out in one's first theology class or one is a PhD candidate (usually meaning one's dissertation topic, the final project before completion and award of the doctorate). In short, the habits and skills of a good undergraduate theology student are transferrable for the rest of life, including for graduate studies (in theology and otherwise).

First, don't forget that the life of the mind and life in the Spirit are not two separate things. Rather, what we do in the library or in our study, or what we do in reading and writing—all these are spiritual exercises or at least can be approached as such. To be sure, these activities do not displace prayer and Scripture reading or meditation. The point is that our studies ought to be integrated into the rhythms of our spiritual lives rather than considered something else that we do. Hence our spiritual disciplines involve rather than parallel our academic and scholarly practices. Put another way: approach the latter as vehicles of the Spirit's formational work in our lives and as means of the Spirit's ongoing renewal of our minds.

Second and relatedly, don't forget that our scholarly activities are academically situated but partaken as part of a community of faith-seeking-understanding. Sometimes, our churches in general are not supportive of our theological questions. Do not switch churches haphazardly but prayerfully and in accompaniment with confidants and mentors. Maybe your church leaders will be open to revising their stances toward theological education. Or maybe God can use you to provide examples of how theological study can support the mission of that church rather than detract from its effectiveness in ministry and the edification of lives. In any case, find conversation partners who can fortify your ecclesial connections and extend the reach of their commitments. The church and its mission are the wider context within which the saving work of God is accomplished in this world. Our theological endeavors ought to be generated from such activities as well as sustain them.

As we make theological progress, we will encounter new perspectives and new dialogue partners. Sometimes the many voices are confusing, and reconnecting often with trusted mentors is important. Along the way, however, we learn to navigate what initially is dissonant, rejecting some but reappropriating others for our purposes and contexts. Those coming from vastly different backgrounds help us ask new questions that our circles deem closed, even as our own perspective might move our new friends to revisit issues that they have not thought to reconsider. Become more adept in contextualizing the perspectives of the many voices you heed. Some of us are ecclesially situated, others academically so, with a few moving back and forth between. Recognizing these factors will help you negotiate what might otherwise be conflicting proposals. We might find ourselves becoming bridges between church and academy. We can bring scholarly perspectives to the church that elevate the engagement of thoughtful members with the important issues of our world. Or we also can mediate practical perspectives to the academy in ways that ensure relevance of theoretical studies with real-world matters. If you often find yourself betwixt and between, whether in relationship to church-academy or church-society, you are in the place where the Holy Spirit can perhaps use you in bridging otherwise separate domains.

Most importantly, maintain a healthy personal lifestyle. If you are single, develop good eating, resting (Sabbath), and exercise habits, and find the social interaction and stimulation all humans need, in church, academy, and society. If you are married, and even more, with children, each couple and family will negotiate these dynamics uniquely. Surely, a man "should love his wife as himself, and a wife should respect her husband" (Eph. 5:33). Certainly also, fathers or mothers who are aspiring scholars and theologians should "not provoke your children to anger, but bring them up in the discipline and instruction of the Lord" (Eph. 6:4). The author of the First Letter to Timothy put it this way with regard to pastoral agents: "If they do not know how to manage their own household, how can they take care of God's church?" (1 Tim. 3:5 CEB). This might be rephrased for those anticipating a theological vocation: if they do not know how to love and care for their spouse and family, how can they be adequate custodians of the theological truths of God's revelation? It thus can be received also as an appropriate extension of an important scriptural and spiritual principle.

The Spirit and the Intellectual Vocation

Not everyone is called to be a professional theologian or to complete a graduate-level course of study in theology. But this book has sought to present every follower and disciple of Jesus as a theologian, whether we self-identify as such or not. Believers in Jesus base their commitments on theological notions, however incipient. If our gifts, aptitudes, and skills set us on the pathway, we might end up with PhDs in theology and perhaps be like Thomas Aquinas. If such a possibility is eventually realized, what do we have to look forward to?

A theologian is merely one who attempts, in faith, to think divine thoughts after God's self-revelation, and in that sense to relate all that we know to that disclosure. This is a lifelong endeavor, as has been repeatedly mentioned. It can be all-captivating: there is much to know and much to relate to a God that, despite the scriptural communication, remains opaque. When we embrace a theological vocation, we realize that we succeed along this path of inquiry not in our own strength but only in the power of the Holy Spirit.

A theologian is thereby also a teacher, one who is in a better position to help others understand otherwise difficult matters about God and God's relationship to the world. This does not mean that we can answer all the

questions posed to us but that we can help others understand why their que-
ries are difficult yet still important. Theological teachers can live out their
vocations in various contexts: interpersonally amid the family and social contexts, and ecclesially in relationship to the churches they frequent or join as
members. In the latter cases, they might be teachers in more formal senses,
in lay educational courses of study or perhaps as providing ministerial leadership in preaching and teaching.

A theologian might also be a professor at any number of educational institutions: secondary, tertiary, or postgraduate. Within the tertiary level, there
are unaccredited start-ups, those accredited at this or that level, or those formally recognized and validated by a range of ecclesial or secular agencies to
offer degrees. Our teaching involves not just lecturing but also opening up
theological pathways for our students. There are mundane tasks such as grad-
ing papers, but doing so in the Spirit helps us to include a comment here or
there that might inspire students to new heights or prompt the imagination
of new possibilities. There will also be collegial and committee work. We
ought to approach such responsibilities as opportunities to further strengthen
programs of study that facilitate the quality and possibility of ever-greater
student learning and transformation.

A theologian will have been trained to research, write, and, hopefully, pub-
lish. Perhaps the dissertation can be turned into a book, or at least aspects of
the dissertation, if not also some of the essays written for doctoral seminars,
can be published in journal articles. In addition, theologians might translate
some of their findings for denominational, church, or popular magazines, or
begin to blog, or write for Web-based venues that might be accessible to
any who roam or surf the Internet. The more theologians put their ideas out
there, whether in print or other media, the more likely they are to be recognized as having something significant to say about issues that matter. So the
more of your videos or recordings of talks are uploaded onto YouTube, the
wider audience your work will engage.

Developing one's scholarly and public voice will lead to invitations to
speak on topics related to your research and ongoing areas of interest. In that
sense, a theologian will inevitably be a consultant of some sort. If all goes well,
you will be adequately and appropriately compensated. As the Scripture says,
"The laborer deserves to be paid" (1 Tim. 5:18b). The reality, though, is that
when participating in God's mission, one sometimes provides consultation,
or accepts speaking engagements, for minimal or no honoraria. Yet there will
continue to be opportunities for you to provide perspective as a recognized
"expert" in areas that you have spent years studying. These would be in academic, church, or other contexts, providing scholarly interpretation and commentary in the former and more practical advice in the latter arenas.

Last but not least, a theologian could develop into a prophetic and public voice for change. This might be a more hazardous vocation since prophets often say unwelcomed things among those they know best. Thus Jesus even warned: "Prophets are not without honor, except in their hometown, and among their own kin, and in their own house" (Mark 6:4). Yet the prophetic vocation, like that of the professional theologian, is not necessarily of one's own choosing but a call and then gift of the Holy Spirit. Because I speak less from experience, I often quote my biblical namesake: "I am no prophet, nor a prophet's son" (Amos 7:14). So if the Spirit should call me in this direction next, I hope I will have the courage to take this step. I pray the same for you.

Discussion Questions

1. Who are the two or three persons—pastors, teachers, or others—whom you would trust to confide in and discuss next steps in your spiritual and theological trek?
2. What kinds of church conferences have you been to? Can you anticipate how academic conferences might be similar, or different?
3. Who are the significant others in your life—parents, siblings, spouses—who might be able to support or would (necessarily) take next steps with you in your theological education? Can you anticipate how your discussions with these persons would go if they have not yet been broached?
4. Can you imagine yourself as a theological teacher, speaker, writer, consultant, or prophet? What excites or scares you about such possibilities?

For Further Reading

Aleshire, Daniel O. *Earthen Vessels: Hopeful Reflections on the Work and Future of Theological Schools*. Grand Rapids: Wm. B. Eerdmans Publishing Co., 2008.

Calian, Carnegie Samuel. *The Ideal Seminary: Pursuing Excellence in Theological Education*. Louisville, KY: Westminster John Knox Press, 2002.

Cetuk, Virginia Samuel. *What to Expect in Seminary: Theological Education as Spiritual Formation*. Nashville: Abingdon Press, 1998.

González, Justo L. *The History of Theological Education*. Nashville: Abingdon Press, 2015.

Hamel, April Vahle, and Jennifer S. Furlong. *The Graduate School Funding Handbook*. 3rd ed. University Park: University of Pennsylvania Press, 2011.

Johns, Cheryl Bridges. *Pentecostal Formation: A Pedagogy among the Oppressed*. Sheffield: Sheffield Academic Press, 1993.

Kibbe, Michael. *From Topic to Thesis: A Guide to Theological Research*. Downers Grove, IL: IVP Academic, 2016.

Mumby, Dave G. *Graduate School: Winning Strategies for Getting In*. 2nd ed. Rigaud, Quebec: Proto Press Publications, 2011.

Pazmiño, Robert W. *Doing Theological Research: An Introductory Guide for Survival in Theological Education*. Eugene, OR: Wipf & Stock, 2009.

Smith, Kevin Gary. *Writing and Research: A Guide for Theological Students*. Cumbria, UK: Langham, 2016.

Yong, Amos. *Spirit-ed Theological Formation: Renewing the Church in the World between the Times*. Forthcoming.

Zacharias, H. Daniel, and Benjamin K. Forrest. *Surviving and Thriving in Seminary: An Academic and Spiritual Handbook*. Bellingham, WA: Lexham Press, 2017.

Acknowledgments

In April 2017, on one of his semiregular visits to Fuller Seminary, Westminster John Knox Press (WJKP) executive editor Robert (Bob) Ratcliff asked to visit with me, and we had a pleasant chat in my office. He invited me to consider some writing initiatives he was involved with at WJKP. I declined since I was already working on three to four manuscripts at that time, one of which is a commentary on the book of Revelation, promised for the end of 2019 for the Belief: A Theological Commentary series that he publishes. But later that week I thought to myself that I had a short and accessible book that could and perhaps ought to be written over the summer of 2017. I drafted a proposal and got an enthusiastic response from Bob and his colleagues at WJKP. Bob then also gave me excellent editorial feedback on the manuscript I submitted. The book you hold in your hands was conceived and executed within the span of the last few months.

I am grateful to the following colleagues who read a draft of the manuscript and in short order provided comments to help me improve it: Christopher (Crip) Stephenson of Lee University, Eric Newberg of Oral Roberts University, and Lisa Millen of University of South Dakota. Samuel H. Hogan, one of Eric's students, also read some sections and gave me valuable perspective. All errors of fact or interpretation remain my own responsibility. My daughter-in-law Neddy Yong also read the manuscript and, as an economics and MBA graduate, gave me realistic but encouraging feedback. Last but not least, my graduate assistant, Nok Kam, helped with the indexes.

As always, my wife, Alma, gave me the space needed in July (2017) for the initial draft of the manuscript to emerge. We were also in the midst of a move from our house to an apartment, which highlights the heights and depths of her sustaining love. Her patience, kindness, and grace are divine gifts that sustain me daily.

This book is dedicated to three individuals at Bethel University, where I had my first long-term, tenure-track teaching appointment (in 1999–2005).

John Herzog was chair of the Biblical and Theological Studies (BTS) Department when I was invited to join the faculty in the late spring of 1999. He welcomed me to the Upper Midwest, helped me to acclimate to Bethel and the historic Swedish pietist ethos of its parent denomination (the Baptist General Conference), guided my initiation into teaching undergraduate theology students and courses, and supported me in every way and at every turn, including championing my various requests to higher administration (see the next paragraph) and finding ways to cover for them. John gave himself to administration of the BTS for the sake of his colleagues. It was because of his selflessness that I was able to write a few books during these years in Minneapolis–St. Paul.

Jay Barnes, now president at Bethel, was provost during my tenure. He supported me as a young theologian through course releases for editorial work and scholarship, J-term exemptions, and the gift of a semester off (in the fall of 2004) so that I could accept the invitation to be a visiting scholar at another university. Although Bethel remains primarily a teaching institution, it is because of the leadership that administrators like Jay have provided over the decades that BTS faculty during, before, and after my time, not to mention colleagues in other departments, have been so productive in their scholarship. Jay made time for me then, and he does also now whenever I get a chance to visit (not as frequently as I would like).

Paul Eddy preceded me at Bethel, but we both had completed our PhD theses in theology of religions about the same time in the late 1990s. Paul is one of those amazingly productive theologians in the BTS, in part underestimated because much of his work is also with and for his pastor and friend (Gregory Boyd, my former colleague also). Paul was doubly busy because he also worked as one of the pastors (with Greg) at Woodland Hills Church, which is why we did not get together for lunch as often as I would have liked. But I consider him a kind of theological soul mate from my Bethel days, with complementary theological proclivities and sensibilities. And he has the demeanor that just makes one—me, at least—enjoy theological friendship.

John, Jay, and Paul are mentors and colleagues who became friends. All young faculty members need such persons in their lives in order to grow in their theological vocation. They are undeserved gifts to me, and I am grateful for their imprint on my life. Thanks, fellas, for helping to make my Bethel years and experiences good memories. It is to you that I dedicate this book.

Glossary

affections/affectivity. Having to do with the feeling dimension of human life, including but not reducible to emotional experience.

affective reason. How our conscious thought processes are subconsciously influenced by our instincts, feelings, emotions, embodied life experiences, desires, and hopes.

Anabaptism. That segment of the Protestant Reformation, also called the Radical Reformation, that practiced adult or believer's baptism following conscious confession of faith and rejected the baptism of infants.

Anglicanism. The Church of England that arose during the Reformation but that sought to find a middle way between the Roman Catholic Church and the Protestants.

Anglican triad. The emphasis on Scripture, tradition, and reason that developed in the Anglican Church and was understood to strike the balance between Catholicism's perceived emphasis on tradition and the Protestant *sola scriptura* approach.

Aristotelianism. The school of philosophy so named after fourth-century BCE thinker Aristotle, who could be said to have tempered the more resolute rationalistic and idealistic thinking of his teacher and predecessor, Plato, with a more empirical approach and orientation.

Calvinism. The system of theology so named after the sixteenth-century French-Swiss Reformer at Geneva, John Calvin, who wrote *Institutes of the Christian Religion* and emphasized the sovereignty and glory of God.

canonical hermeneutics. An approach to the interpretation of the Bible that emphasizes reading one portion or section in light of the full collection of texts recognized as sacred (in the Protestant tradition, sixty-six books together from Genesis to Revelation).

Cartesianism. A philosophical system based on the ideas of the sixteenth-century Frenchman René Descartes and his successors, emphasizing the use of reason and its capacity to construct indubitable and thereby presumed necessary foundations for human thinking.

charisma. Describes organizational forms that are more dynamically shaped by leadership with personal qualities that appeal to and motivate the efforts of followers to achieve organizational goals.

charismatic renewal. Usually refers to movements within mainline Protestant, Roman Catholic, and Eastern Orthodox churches that come to accept the manifestation of the spiritual gifts of the Holy Spirit as part of the life of their communities and congregations.

common-sensism. An eighteenth- and nineteenth-century philosophical school that reacted to the idealistic and rationalistic philosophies of the early modern period and urged the dependence and reliability of perception and experience as understood by ordinary people.

conservativism. A way of life and thinking that privileges what has been handed down by tradition beforehand, especially the tradition of one's immediate community, and is more cautious about introducing changes to these established conventions.

dialectics. A mode of reasoning that goes back and forth between two or more positions, usually striving for resolution but content to remain in tension until or unless consensus emerges.

Eastern Orthodoxy. The tradition of churches that traces its lineage to the Greek-speaking East, in contrast to the Latin-speaking Roman Catholic Church, emphasizing the centrality of the liturgy for the church's belief and practices.

ecumenism. The principle regarding the unity of all churches worldwide, including the related programs and initiatives devoted to implementing such a vision of the church.

egalitarianism. The idea that all people are equal, with equal rights and responsibilities, a notion that Christian churches have applied particularly to the equality of men and women.

empiricism. The belief that all knowledge derives from sense experience and is thus best accumulated via experimental methods.

Enlightenment. A philosophic movement in eighteenth-century Europe, also known as the Age of Reason, which produced a way of thinking that sought to subordinate received religious authorities to rational and scientific approaches.

epistemology. The area of study about how we know and how we justify our knowing and knowledge.

eschatology. The area of study that concerns the *eschaton*, Greek for the last things, end times, or events at the end of the world as we know it.

evangelicalism. A broad movement of generally conservative Protestants who see themselves distinct from mainline Protestant denominations considered to be more liberal in beliefs and practices.

exegesis. In hermeneutics, the idea that the meaning of texts ought to be derived from within texts rather than to be imposed on them from the outside (by our biases or presuppositions).

experience. As understood in this book, constituted by historical lives embedded in and shaped by (in no particular order) race/ethnicity, gender, dis/ability, privilege-oppression, religion, and other social factors.

globalization. The gradual internationalization of our lives, both our capacity to have wider and wider influence but also the impact of forces from the other side of the world on our activities and decisions.

hermeneutical spiral. The notion that our reading of texts transforms what and how we think even as there is acknowledgment that the perspectives we bring to our reading also provide lenses for our interpretation, and back and forth.

hermeneutics. The art or rules of interpretation of texts.

historical criticism. Reading texts while asking and attending to questions of the world *behind* the text, including who the authors were, what were the circumstances in which they wrote, what their motivations were, within what constraints they operate, and so forth.

idealism. The philosophical system asserting that reality is mind-dependent, ultimately, or that ideas are foundational and prior to material realities.

indigenous traditions. Local cultures, such as Native American or Aboriginal groups, including their religious lives and practices, that have been transmitted over the millennia by popular means.

interdisciplinarity. As used in this book, calling attention to how Christian theology involves multiple disciplinary perspectives and methods, from biblical to historical to those that engage with and help us understand human society and the wider creation in all its complexity.

intersectionality. Related to the interconnected nature of group or personal identity aspects such as race, class, gender, and sexuality, which also often are the bases for social privileges and discrimination.

intersubjectivity. The process of interpersonal engagement whereby persons are subjects (of their own thinking) and objects (of another's interaction) simultaneously, and the emerging consensus that arrives out of such interface that is beyond mere subjectivity or mere objectivity.

Kantianism. A philosophical system related to the achievements of Enlightenment German thinker Immanuel Kant, which remain far-reaching even in our present late-modern or postmodern time.

liberalism. A way and life view that prioritizes tolerance and is therefore more insistent on the rights of all to have their own convictions and the opportunity to promote those views while respecting others with differing opinions.

literary hermeneutics. An approach to the interpretation of Scripture that emphasizes features of the text such as genre, plot, narrative, and so forth.

liturgy/liturgical. The worship performed by religious or church groups, variously scripted, to facilitate interaction with God.

metaphysics. Philosophical areas of study that involve primordial notions and abstract concepts like being, knowing, change, and so forth.

Methodism. The movement launched by John and Charles Wesley's Holy Club that over time became a mainline Protestant church and denomination.

narrative hermeneutics. An approach to the interpretation of Scripture that emphasizes the dramatic character of sacred texts and seeks to understand doctrinal or other teachings in light of the stories of the Bible.

Neoplatonism. A philosophical movement in the second and following centuries of the Christian era that featured an updating and expansion of Plato's philosophical idealism.

objectivity. The philosophical and epistemological concern that our knowing is based on facts and actualities rather than our perceived (subjective) whims and fancies.

ontology. The study of the nature of things, or of the being of things or realities.

Orthodox Christianity. Mostly synonymous with Eastern Orthodoxy.

orthodoxy. Concerned with or regarding the received or approved teachings of a group, thus in the case of Christianity, its correct doctrines as opposed to misguided heresies (false views).

Pentecost, Day of. The Acts 2 account about the outpouring of the Holy Spirit and the ensuing speaking or hearing in the many languages of the people groups from around the Mediterranean region who were then gathered in Jerusalem.

Pentecostalism. A modern-day movement of those for whom speaking in tongues is considered an ongoing sign of the Holy Spirit's continued work in the world.

Pietists/pietism. A movement (pietism) within the Christian tradition whose members (pietists) have historically emphasized the importance of a personal religious life that is heartfelt, contrasting with those who emphasize reason (rationalists) and a religiosity of doctrines and ideas (scholastics).

Platonism. The school of philosophy so named after the fourth-century BCE thinker Plato, who promoted a more idealistic interpretation of the world and its realities, including God.

pneumatology. The study of or teaching about *Pneuma*, or in Christian theological terms, the Holy Spirit.

post-Christendom. A way of understanding present and more recent times after the end of that period in the Western world, Christendom, when the Christian church had political power and was formally aligned with the state.

post-Christianity. A way of understanding our contemporary secular Western context, when Christian faith is not as widely accepted across culture and society as in previous centuries.

postcolonialism. A way of understanding our contemporary world, where colonized nations have become autonomous (rather than being ruled by Europeans) and sought to develop their own cultures and governments.

postmodernism. A way of understanding our present era, which seeks to deemphasize modern, Enlightenment rationality and allow for more diverse approaches to knowing and thinking.

practical reason. How action and activity are part of human reasoning processes and how the latter cannot be reduced to theoretical or speculative reason only.

pragmatism. A philosophical school emphasizing that the meanings of beliefs are clarified in their practical applications.

primitivism. A set of religious sensibilities holding that the older or more ancient a tradition of beliefs and practices is, the more reliable and trustworthy it may be.

Protestantism. The family of churches that resulted from the sixteenth-century Reformation of the Roman Catholic Church.

Radical Reformation. A movement of Protestants who challenged the sacramentalism of the primary sixteenth-century Reformers and sought to limit church membership only to believers baptized not as infants but as adults, based on their confession of faith.

rationalism. The belief that only human reasoning ought to trump so-called experience and take precedence over what has been handed down by religious or traditional authorities.

Reformation. The movement of protests seeking to reform the Roman Catholic Church in the first half of the sixteenth century.

Renaissance. A period in European intellectual and cultural history from the fourteenth to the seventeenth century that sought to retrieve ancient sources in order to cultivate a more complete understanding of humanity.

restorationism. Movements that seek to retrieve and reappropriate the beliefs and practices of the early church for later times.

Roman Catholicism. The Western Church, originally Latin in practice and under the authority of the pope, that formed the setting for the Protestant reforms of the sixteenth century.

sacraments. The practices or ceremonies of the church, especially baptism in water and the Eucharist, or the Lord's Supper (for Protestants; Catholics have others), that are believed to be mediators of divine grace according to the promises of Scripture.

scholasticism. A system of theology and philosophy prominent in medieval European universities, featuring the resurgence of Aristotelian logic and methods.

scientism. An approach holding that the scientific method is sufficient to lead to truth in all spheres of knowledge.

subjectivity. The sense of being and knowing based on personal feelings, desires, tastes, opinions, and the like.

theodicy. Arguments used to defend God's goodness and justice in the face of suffering and evil.

Thomism. The system of theology based on Thomas Aquinas's ideas.

tradition. As understood in this book, refers to the ecclesial or church streams that inform Christian life, reflection, theologizing, and experience, intertwined with sociohistorical contexts and circumstances.

Trinity. One of the central teachings of the Christian faith, about God existing as Father, Son, and Holy Spirit.

Wesleyanism. The system of theology based on John Wesley's teachings.

Wesleyan quadrilateral. Emphasis on Scripture, tradition, reason, and experience as sources of theology, adapted from John Wesley's approach.

world Christianity. Christianity as it has spread around the world, including its Asian, African, and Latin American expressions, which are significantly different from Western forms.

Index of Scripture

OLD TESTAMENT

Genesis
1:2	49
1:27	71
2:7	49
50:20	72

2 Samuel
24:1–2	19

1 Kings
19:12	61

1 Chronicles
21:1	19

Job
33:4	49
34:14–15	49

Psalms
95:7–11	18
104:29–30	49

Isaiah
40:13	49
55:8–9	49
61:1–2	62

Daniel
1:4	48

Joel
2:28–32	24

Amos
7:14	119

NEW TESTAMENT

Matthew
5:23–24	82
16:18	63
25:31–46	71
27:5	22
28:19–20	85

Mark
6:4	119

Luke
4:18–19	62
10:27	8, 63
12:48	72

John
1:1–14	41
1:14	16
10:10	73
10:27	73
13:34–35	86
14:6	67
14:26	106
15:26	106
16:13	87
16:13–14	106
18:38	67
20:30–31	22

Acts
1:8	61
1:16–18	22
2	24, 104
2:11	50
2:14–21	24
2:17	37, 74
2:33	105
2:37–38	105
2:42	81
2:44	86
2:47	86
7:22	48
8:26–40	33
10:38	62
17:2	97
17:11	36
17:17	97
18:4	97
19:8–9	97

Romans
1–11	70
1:4	104
1:20	69
5:5	75, 106
8:20–23	86
8:26	86–87, 107
8:28	72
9	73
11:33	75–76
12–16	70
12:1	70
12:2	48
12:6–7	71
14:17	71

1 Corinthians

1:19–31	49
2:4–5	49
2:6	49
2:7–8	49
2:10–13	49
2:11	49
2:14–16	49
3:16	71
6:19	71
12	61
12:10	72
12:12–13	105
12:13	62
13:12	6
14:29	96
15:3–4	36
15:28	106

2 Corinthians

1:22	75
3:6	23
4:13	36
5:5	75
5:7	61
10:4–5	48–49
13:13	29

Galatians

3:28	57
5:22–23	71

Ephesians

1:13–14	75
3:20	63
5:33	117
6:4	117

Colossians

1:8	75
1:9–10	75
1:15–18	75
2:8	49
3:11	57
3:17	91

1 Thessalonians

5:17	69

1 Timothy

3:5	117
5:18	118

2 Timothy

3:15–17	21
3:16	36

Titus

3:5	105

Hebrews

3:7–11	18
4:12	23
11:6	109

James

1:27	81

2 Peter

1:21	17
3:12	87

1 John

1:1	16
3:2	74
4:2–3	72

Jude

3	36

Revelation

2:7	22
2:11	22
2:17	22
2:29	22
3:6	22
3:13	22
3:22	22
7:9	83

Index of Subjects and Names

ableism, 59
aesthetics, 53
affections/affectivity, 19–20, 44, 46,
    60, 68
agnosticism, 44, 59, 75
Albert the Great, 4
American Academy of Religion, 114
Anabaptism, 31
Anglican triad, 8–9, 27, 39
Anglicanism, 8, 31, 60
Anselm, 69
Antony the Great, 2
Apocrypha, 3, 35
apologetics, 7, 84, 106
apostolicity, 85–87
Aquinas. *See* Thomas Aquinas
Aristotelianism, 5, 9, 39–42, 83
Aristotle, 40
arts, 46
ascetism, 2–3, 61
Assemblies of God, 102
Athanasius, 2
atheists, 59
Augustine of Hippo, 106

Basil of Caesarea, 2
Basil the Elder, 2
Buddhism, 42, 83–84

Calvinism, 6, 7
Cappadocians, 2–3, 106
carnality, 3
Cartesianism, 43–44
catholicity, 33–35, 83–85
Chalcedon, 28

charismatic movements, 30–31
charisms, 27–32, 61–62, 71–72, 96,
    104, 113
children, 54, 60, 68, 85
Christendom, 35, 47
Christianity, world, 27, 84
Christology, 16, 37, 74, 79, 87
church
    councils of, 28
    and doctrine, 78–80
    growth of, 86
    as holy, 80–83
    marks of the, 34, 37, 77
    mission of, 116
    multicultural, 83
colonialism, 33, 45, 47
colorblindness, 58
common-sensism, 44, 45
communion, 81
confessionalism, 29–30
confessions, 36, 78
Confucianism, 42, 83–84
consciousness, 54
    historical, 48
conservatism, 32, 35–36, 43, 56, 61, 95
Constantinopolitan creed, 28
contextuality, 35–37
contextualization, 48, 116
Copernicus, Nicolaus, 42
council, 28
    of Constantinople, 28
    ecumenical, 28–29, 41
    Second Vatican, 29
    of Trent, 31
creativity, 48, 73, 90

creeds, 5, 28–31, 34, 36, 41, 61, 78–80, 106, 108
  Chalcedonian, 79
  Constantinopolitan, 28
  conciliar, 36
  ecclesial, 78
  ecumenical, 34
  Nicene, 28, 106
criticism,
  canonical,17–18
  historical, 17
  intertextual, 18–19
  literary, 19
Crusades, 9
cultures, 83–85

Daoism, 42, 83–84
death, 2–3, 68, 104
Descartes, René, 43–44
Deutronomic historian, 36
devotion, 23
dialectic, 27
dialogue, 97, 116
digitization, 34
disability, 46, 56, 58
discernment, spiritual, 72–73
discipleship, 60
discipline, spiritual, 96–98
dissertation, 115, 118
diversity, 50, 77, 78, 85
doctrine, 78–80
dualism, subject-object, 44

Easter, xi, 103, 104
Eastern Orthodox Christianity, 8, 27–29, 31, 33, 41–42
ecclesia, sociality of, 80–83
ecumenism, 28–29, 32, 34, 36–37, 41, 78
education, 95
  graduate, 115–117
  theological, 69, 111–13
egalitarianism, 57–58
election, 6
embodiment, 7, 41, 42, 46
emotion, 20, 44, 46
empiricism, 7, 41–44
encounter
  interreligious, 40, 84

Muslim-Christian, 9–10, 40
  spiritual, 9, 16, 59–61, 68, 70
Enlightenment, 42–48
enthusiasm, 7, 61
environment, 87, 94
epiclesis, 29
epistemology, 45
eschatology, 50, 74–78, 80–81, 83, 87, 106
ethnicity, 8, 46, 53, 57–58
ethnocentrism, 59
Eucharist, or Lord's Supper, 5, 60, 81
Evangelical Theological Society, 114
evangelicalism, 32, 35–36, 60, 102, 114
Evangelische Kirche in Deutschland, 32
exile, 17, 19, 36, 82
experience, 39–42, 44–45, 53–63, 69–71, 75, 82, 96–97, 101–108, 111, 114–115, 119, 122
experientialism, 7

faith, 16, 20
faith-seeking-understanding, 20, 68, 74, 108, 116
feminism, 46
finitude, 7
freedom, 73, 86
  Baptistic, 61
  of conscience, 34
  of religion, 34

Galileo, Galilei, 42–43,
gifts, charismatic or spiritual. *See* charisms
globalization, 35, 45, 47
Gnosticism, 41
God, image of, 71
  knowing, 68–70
  love of, 107
  loving, 68–70
  worshiping, 108
good, common, 84
grace, 7
  divine, 68
  prevenient, 6
Gregory of Nazianzus, 2
Gregory of Nyssa, 2, 106
guilds, academic, 113–115

Hades, 3, 63

healing, 60–62
health, 117
heavens, new, 87
Heber, Reginald, 106
heliocentrism, 43
hermeneutics, 16–22, 79
Hinduism, 42, 59, 83, 84
history
  of Christianity, 30
  of effects, 20, 27
  intellectual, 104
  reception, 20, 27
holiness, 3, 6, 31, 61, 83
Holy Spirit, 6–7, 9–10, 24–25, 29, 35,
    60, 80, 91, 99, 105
  communion of, 81
  discernment of, 72–73
  experience of, 102
  filled with, 61, 74, 87
  fruits of, 71
  gifts of, 71
  life in, 67, 116
  starting with, 102–103
homosexuality, 58
hope, 60, 68, 74–75, 84, 86
hospitality, 109
Hume, David, 44

iconography, 60
idealism, 41–42
imagination, 113, 114, 118
  sacramental, 60
  theological, 55, 69
immortality, of the soul, 2
impairments, 58, 82
imperative, categorical, 44, 54
incarnation, 4, 37, 41, 71, 79, 83,
    104
individualism, 47
infinity, 108, 120
institutions, 27–30
integration, theological, 94–96
interdisciplinarity, 94
interreligious interactions, 84–85
intersectionality, 53, 56–59, 61
intersex, 58
intersubjectivity, 50, 77
intertextuality, 18
irrationalism, postmodern, 45–48

Jesus Christ, 3–4, 7–8, 10, 16, 20–22, 28,
    36–37, 57, 59–60, 62–63, 67, 71–75, 79,
    82–83, 85–87, 89, 91, 104–106, 108,
    117, 119
Jews, 59
Joint Declaration on the Doctrine of Justifi-
    cation, 32
journey, spiritual, 94
justice, 45, 84
justification, 82

Kant, Immanuel, 44

LaHaye, Tim, 74
Leo XIII, Pope, 5
life after death, 22, 68
liturgy, 29, 30, 41
Locke, John, 43–44
Logos, 1, 16, 41
love
  of God, 107
  of neighbor, 81
  Trinitarian, 107

Macrina, 2–4, 9
magisterium, 29–30
meditation, contemplative, 69, 91
memory, 54
metanarrative, 19, 46, 48
metaphysics, 20, 37
metarationality, 46
method
  empirical, 47
  historical, 16
  scientific, 43, 45
Methodism, 32
migration, 34, 45, 47
miracle, 61
mission, 71, 85–87
monotheism, 84, 106
morality, 53
multiculturality, 84
Muslims, 59, 109
mystery, 5, 71, 79, 80, 107

narrative, 18–20, 23
  incarnational, 63
  local, 46
  pentecostal, 63

National Association of Evangelicals, 32
neighbors
    loving, 70–72, 81
    reconciliation with, 82
    serving, 70–72
Neoplatonism, 41
Nicaea, 28, 77

objectivity, 46, 50
Orthodox Christianity. *See* Eastern
    Orthodox Christianity
orthodoxy, 33–34

passion, 44
patriarchalism, 46, 59
Pentecost, 24, 50, 74, 83, 95, 97, 101,
    103–106
Pentecostalism, 30–31, 37, 41
perfection, 7, 31, 61
perseverance, 6
philosophy, 104
Pietism, 6, 8, 23–24
Pius V, Pope, 4
Plato, 2–3, 40–42, 83
Platonism, 41–42
pluralism, 50, 85
pneumatology, 101, 105
postcolonialism, 45–47
postmodernism, 45–48, 50
practices, 10
    Christian, 67
    ecclesial, 77–78, 81
    spiritual, 70, 89
pragmatism, 23–24
prayer, 69, 72
preaching, 60, 81, 118
presentation, scholarly, 114
primitivism, 30
proclamation, 60
professoriate, 118
programs, online, 90–91
    Doctor of Ministry, 113
    Doctor of Missiology, 113
    Doctor of Theology, 112
prophecy, 17, 29, 30, 32, 119
Protestantism, 33
publication, scholarly, 114–115, 118
purification, 3

quadrilateral, xi, 8–9, 14–15, 25, 27–28,
    39–40, 53, 62, 97

race/racism, 46, 59
rationalism, 41, 43–44
rationality, 8, 40–42, 44–48, 50, 56, 62,
    74–77
    affective, 46
    Christian, 62
    Enlightenment, 47
    eschatological, 74–77
    liturgical, 39
    modern, 56
    multiconversational, 50
    practical, 44
    scientific, 46–47
    scriptural, 48
Realism, Common Sense, 44
reason, 47
    affective, 44
    Enlightenment, 46
    and faith, 40
    universal, 42–45
reconciliation, 82
redemption, 59–61
Reformation, 23, 60
    Radical, 30–31, 34
regeneration, 7
reign (kingdom) of God, 37, 50, 63, 73
relativism, 47–48
religion, study of, 94
Renaissance, 23, 30
renewal, 6, 30, 31, 37, 63, 80, 87, 105, 116
research paper/writing, 92–94
resurrection, 2–4, 16, 104, 108
restorationism, 23, 30
revelation, 30, 80, 117
    from above, 40
    from below, 40
review, book, 115
    peer, 90, 96
revival, 31
revolution, scientific, 42–45
righteousness, 84
Roman Catholicism, 6, 28–32, 42

sacraments, 41
salvation, 6, 25, 61, 82

sanctification, 3, 7, 25, 82
scholarship, financial, 114
Scholasticism, 39, 83
sciences
    evolutionary, 95
    modern, 45
    political, 94
Scripture, 36, 97
second coming, 74
Second Vatican Council, 29
Second War World, 45
secularization, 35
seminaries, 112
sexism, 59
signs and wonders, 61
sin, 7, 59–61, 63, 68, 79, 105
    of commission, 7
    of omission, 7
skepticism, 43–44
socialization, 53–56
society, academic, 114
Society for Pentecostal Studies, 103
Society of Biblical Literature, 114
Socrates, 2
sola scriptura, 30–31, 35
soul, 2–3, 8, 23, 43, 60–61,63, 79, 87, 109,
    122
spirituality, 60, 67–69, 89
    Christian, 74, 77
    pentecostal, 104
suffering, 69
subjectivity, 46, 50
superstition, 43
system, cultural-linguistic, 50

teachers, 118
telecommunication, 45
theism, 44
theodicy, 69

theologian
    lay, 1, 2–4
    pastoral, 6–8
    practical, 6–8
    professional, 1, 4–6, 8, 68–69, 111–119
theologizing, 96–98, 103–105, 108
theology, 1
    political, 82, 94
    of religions, 94
    study of, 97, 111–113
    truth of, 67
Thomas Aquinas, 1, 4–9, 40, 83, 117
Torah, 36
traditions, 97
    Eastern Orthodox, 105
    ecclesial, 27, 31–32, 34–35, 50
    Roman Catholic, 105
transgender, 58
translation, 83
Trinitarianism, 10, 29
Trinity, 28
truth, 20, 87

unconscious, 45
unity, ecclesial, 78–80
university, 45, 94–96

vocation, intellectual, 117–119

Wesley, Charles, 6
Wesley, John, 6–8, 10, 31
Wesley, Susanna, 6
Wesleyan Holiness movement, 9
Wesleyan quadrilateral. *See* quadrilateral
Wisdom literature, 36
witness, 83–85
wonder, 69, 75
works, 21
world, 68, 81, 84

Made in the USA
San Bernardino, CA
05 September 2019